A History of Theatres & Performers in Herefordshire

A History of Theatres & Performers in Herefordshire

by
Robin Haig

Logaston Press

LOGASTON PRESS
Little Logaston Woonton Almeley
Herefordshire HR3 6QH

Published by Logaston Press 2002
.Copyright © Robin Haig 2002

ISBN 1 873827 48 2

Set in Times and Baskerville by Logaston Press
and printed in Great Britain by
Bell & Bain Ltd., Glasgow

*Front Cover: Broad Street, Hereford, by Lewis Powell, 1873. The Corn
Exchange, later The Kemble Theatre, is shown on the left
Rear Cover: The Courtyard Centre for the Arts*

Contents

Acknowledgements

I would like to acknowledge my deep obligation to the following people who have helped me in the course of my researches for this book: Miss Hubbard and the staff at the Hereford Record Office, and Robin Hill and the staff of the Hereford County Library; Derek Foxton, who has kindly allowed me to reproduce photographs from his collection as well as showing me other relevant documents in his possession; and from Peter Siddons, Paul Ranger, Gina Grainger, Ruth Richardson, Andrew Foley, Basil Butcher, Graham Sprackling, Jonathan Stone, Suz Winspear; and Mike Tomkins, George Powell, Geoff Alcock and many other members of the various amateur dramatic societies of the county.

For providing and giving permission to use illustrations I wish to thank the following who retain copyright: Mr. R.I. Macadie for the front cover illustration of Broad Street, along with Glenn Howells Architects and photographer Rod Dorling for the photograph of The Courtyard Centre for the Arts on the rear cover; Ian Howie p2; The Mander and Mitchenson Theatre Collection p.14; Victoria & Albert Museum, London & Bridgeman Art Library p.15; The British Museum p.25; Herefordshire Heritage Services, Herefordshire Museum pp.21, 22, 34, 50; Cheltenham Art Gallery p.23; a private collection, England p.28; Finsbury Local History Collection, Islington Libraries p.45; Logaston Press pp.29, 53, 85, 86, 93 (with thanks to Mr. and Mrs. Beeden of the Croase for providing access to the room), 100; Derek Foxton Collection pp.83, 101, 103, 106, 117 (top), 119 (in conjunction with Helen Wallace), 124 (in conjunction with Philip Cowal), 128; and the NMR (English Heritage), Swindon p.121 (Crown copyright material is reproduced by permission of English Heritage acting under licence from the Controller of Her Majesty's Stationery Office).

Introduction

'Someone should compile and publish a full account of Hereford's part in drama from the earliest times', wrote Theodore Hannam-Clark, author of *Drama in Gloucestershire*, in a letter to the *Hereford Times* in 1931. After 70 years, here is an account which, if not full, at least gives some idea of the history of drama in the county.

Boasting connections with David Garrick, Sarah Siddons and John Philip Kemble, not to mention Nell Gwyn, Hereford has a theatrical heritage to be proud of. Admittedly Garrick, though born in Hereford, never returned to the city in later life. Nell Gwyn, probably born in a house in Gwynne Street, Hereford, did not return either. Roger Kemble, though, had much closer ties with the city; born in Hereford, he was the manager of a company of strolling players which toured all over the region, performing regularly throughout the county with members of his family, two of whom—John Philip Kemble and Sarah Siddons—rose to the heights of their profession.

Long before the age of Garrick and Kemble, the guilds in mediaeval Hereford would stage mystery plays or pageants at the feast of Corpus Christi, while the people had their own mummers plays. Later on, from the 1580s, bands of noblemens' travelling players used to visit Hereford and Leominster. In the 18th century companies of strolling players—some more respectable than others—began to tour through Herefordshire, playing in barns or inn yards; frowned upon by the law, they were officially consigned, until 1788, to the category of rogues and vagabonds. By the mid-century, though, Hereford, Leominster, Kington, Ross, Ledbury and Bromyard all received visits from John Ward and his company of players, later to come under the management of Roger Kemble. Theatregoing increased in popularity in the course of the 18th century, and the first Hereford Theatre, built in 1786, flourished under the management of the genial Irishman John Boles Watson. But habits changed, and by the mid-19th century theatregoing had gone out of fashion; the Hereford Theatre was finally demolished in 1858, to be replaced by the Corn Exchange. Later on, though, in 1911, the Corn Exchange was itself revamped to become the Kemble Theatre.

Over the centuries the county has seen all kinds of live entertainment in its public buildings and theatres, inns, taverns, music halls, assembly rooms and coffee houses—from a Victorian music hall artiste burning copies of the *Hereford Times* on his nose, to an Elephant versus Man football match in which the captain of the Leominster Football Team competed against the centre forward elephant of Sanger's Circus. The story continues up to the present day, with the opening of the Courtyard Theatre in 1998, and concludes with a look at some of the theatre companies and amateur dramatic societies in the county today.

THE IRON ROOM,
PEMBRIDGE.

—

A Musical

AND

THEATRICAL

Entertainment

WILL (D.V.) BE GIVEN

ON THURSDAY,

January 23, 1902.

Doors open at 7,30 p.m.   *To commence at 8 p.m.*

ADMISSION :

Front Seats (Reserved) - - - **2s. 6d.**

Second Seats - - - - - - **1s.**

Back Seats - - - - - - - **6d.**

Tickets can be obtained from Mrs. CHESTER, The Steps.

THE ORPHANS' PRINTING PRESS. LEOMINSTER.

CHAPTER I
Early Drama and Popular Entertainment

From the early middle ages up until the Reformation, sacred drama in the form of morality or allegorical plays, saints' plays, and, in the later middle ages, elaborate performances of mystery plays, formed a constant part of the religious year.

At parish level, the feast day of the saint to whom the church was dedicated would be celebrated with plays as well as services and markets; guilds, too, would celebrate the feast days of their patron saints. Very little is known about these saints' plays, most of which were destroyed at the Reformation; in France, by contrast over 100 are still extant. However, the medieval Church's attitude to drama was not always favourable. In Hereford in 1348 Bishop John Trilleck forbade the performance of plays and interludes in church because of their offensive humour and rude language (an interlude, in this context, probably signified simply a short play).

Generally, however, the Church found that drama was a powerful way of conveying the great religious truths to the laity. In the early 14th century the feast of Corpus Christi was added to the calendar; on this day, bread and wine would be borne through the streets accompanied by a procession of civic dignitaries and craft guilds, with a series of representations of biblical scenes organized by the guilds. These plays and pageants were enormously popular, and by the end of the 14th century had evolved into the cycles of mystery plays, the earliest of which is recorded in York in 1376. These great cycles—the York cycle contained as many as 48 separate plays—were arguably the most truly popular theatre of all time. They were gigantic community projects in which many hundreds of people would take part; in York at one time a quarter of the population of 8,000 were involved in some way. In York and probably in other cities as well, the plays were performed on pageant carts, pulled along the processional route to the cathedral and stopping at an assigned place where the play would be performed. The cycle of plays embraced the complete Christian view of mankind; and still today, with their sonorous language, they have extraordinary dramatic power. In places they are also very funny, with shepherds in the fields stealing sheep, and an incompetent Noah berated by his harridan wife, clearly the least suitable couple for God to save from the flood.

Though only four cycles of mystery plays are still in existence, each city had its own version, with texts provided by local authors, and there was intense competition to produce the most spectacular plays. Evidence for the mystery plays performed in Hereford is scanty as few civic records have survived; in 1830 the town hall's cleaner was convicted of selling old documents to local merchants as scrap paper in which to wrap goods, and a large part of the *Mayor's Book*, which would have contained records of the Corpus Christi pageants, was lost. The remaining part, however, does contain details of plays being performed at the inauguration of the shrine of St. Thomas Cantilupe. Quite what form the Hereford plays or pageants would have taken is obscure. A pageant performed in 1503 in Hereford as part of the Corpus Christi procession was said to be 'a dumb show only', and probably consisted of static tableaux rather than plays. In this procession, each guild was assigned its own tableau or play, which in a few cases had some relation to its craft. There were 27 plays in all, five of which dealt with Old Testament

Lucifer, Lighthouse and Gabriel—the mystery play performed at Dore Abbey in May 2002 by the Mad Dog Theatre Company

2

subjects, 20 with the life of Christ and two others whose relevance is obscure. The Tanners performed the story of Shrove Thursday, the Carpenters *Noye Ship*, the Chaundelers *Abraham and Isaac*, the Vintners *The Nativity of Our Lord*, the Tailors *The Three Kings*, the Butchers *The Taking of our Lord*, the Gardeners *The Castle of Israel and the tomb of Christ*, the Dyers *Jesus hanging on the Cross*, and the Barbers *Joseph of Arimathea*. In the early decades of the 16th century the Corpus Christi pageants in Hereford lapsed altogether, and by 1548, when the feast was expunged from the calendar by a reformed church suspicious of such Catholic survivals, indeed suspicious of all theatre as being ungodly and lacking in piety, the pageants had already been 'omytted and Surseassed'.

At the same time as this initial growth of religious drama came an increase in civic pageantry. When Henry VII came to Hereford in 1486 during his first provincial progress, he was greeted with a ceremonial pageant in three parts; first, on the king's entry into the city, came a pageant and speech by St. George; at the market place was another pageant, with a speech given by King Ethelbert. Finally, at the entrance to the cathedral, the king was greeted with a third pageant, this time with a speech by the Virgin Mary.

Alongside this sacred drama and civic pageantry, one can discern faint glimpses of a lively tradition of popular revelry, obliterated from the 1580s onwards by a disapproving church. Much of it was connected with the religious cycle of feast days and holy days, particularly the feasts of Christmastide, Shrovetide, and Whitsuntide. Shrovetide, the period before Lent ending on Shrove Tuesday, was the season for carnivals, a time for revelry and riotous amusement providing some last-minute merrymaking before the self-denial of Lent. During the Reformation, the church was ruthless in its suppression of this perceived ungodliness. In 1586 Bishop Westfaling instituted an enquiry to investigate 'whether any Lords of Misrule [mock dignitaries appointed to oversee the seasonal festivities], daunters, players or any other disguised persons [i.e. dressed to perform] do dance, or play any other unseemly parts in the church, church-yard, or chapel-yard, or whether there are any players or common drinking kept in church or church-yards'. Illicit revellers were usually reported by the churwardens during episcopal visitations of the diocese, and would be summoned to appear before the consistory court. If found guilty they would either be pardoned or made to confess in church dressed in penitential garb; if they did not appear, they would be excommunicated. Herefordshire is particularly rich in records of these consistory court prosecutions, most of which concern dancing, morris dancing, playing music or, occasionally, acting in plays. In Leominster,

3

for example, Thomas Wauclen of Kingsland was accused in 1617 of 'acting a play upon the sabath daie at tyme of evening praier'; and in November 1618 a Ledbury innkeeper, Edward Hall, 'the actor and morrice dauncer', was prosecuted by the consistory court, 'having gone out of the parish to other places with a gun and drum both in the night to the disturbance of the king's subjects'.

In 1586 a group of men in Cradley were accused of another form of carnival revelry, which involved carrying a man sitting on a colestaff — a mock throne carried shoulder-high—to the blowing of horns and throwing of grains, 'with such other like fantastical toyes'. This custom, which involved carrying an offender through the village to general derision, was a common punishment for those who refused to give money to the Lord of Misrule. As the puritan Philip Stubbs noted, 'And who will not shew himself buxome to them, and give money for theses the Devils Cogizances, they shall be mocked, and flouted shamefullie. Yea, and many times carried upon a Cowlestaffe'. (This type of noisy uproar, or 'rough music', took place in most Christian countries on Shrovetide, as shown vividly in Brueghel's painting *The Battle Between Carnival and Lent*, where Carnival is riding on a hogshead of wine,

Early instrumental music

4

Riding the colestaff to 'rough music'

wearing a meat pie as his crown, while his followers make 'rough music' by beating on pots.) Other Shrovetide celebrations came to light in Bosbury in 1589, where a certain Richard Kent was excommunicated when he failed to appear in court accused of going 'a-hodiwinking' (a game apparently similar to Blind Man's Buff) on Shrove Sunday. Lords and Ladies of Misrule were appointed during the major festivals, and possibly at other times of year too; thus in September 1619 the church authorities accused two people in Welsh Newton of illicit activities: William Rice, 'detected for Lord of Misrule', and Denise Watkins, 'detected for Lady of Misrule'. This unfortunate pair also failed to appear before the court, and were consequently excommunicated.

There were many prosecutions for playing music; in Stretton Grandison in 1616, 'Richardus Perks, a minstrel' was prosecuted for 'playeing on saboth daies in the parish of Stretton gransham and bringing his tabor into the church at divine service and for unreverent behavinge upon admonition given him'. Even more reprehensible behaviour was shown by a man prosecuted in Welsh Newton in 1619 'for playing on his instrument in welshe newton in eveninge prayer tyme & beynge demaunded by the churchwardens & sworne men why he did not come to church he answered them that if they would bring the church to the place where they played they would come to church'. The county in fact was well known for its music; John Aubrey wrote that 'in Herefordshire & parts of the Marches of Wales, the Tabor and Pipe were exceeding common; many beggars begged with it; and the Peasants danced to it in the Churchyard on Holydayes and Holyday-eves'.

Most of this music would probably have been associated with morris dancing, for which Herefordshire was particularly famous. According to 'Old Meg of Herefordshire', writing in 1609, 'Herefordshire for a Morris Daunce puts downe, not onely all Kent, but verie near three quarters of Christendom'. There were certain parishes in the county where it was especially popular; in Withington and Yazor there were elaborate prose-cutions of large groups of morris dancers on a few occasions, while in Tedstone Delamere there were frequent prosecutions of individuals, such as Miles Conney, who was accused in 1602 of 'profaning the sabbath day and dancing and revelling with morris dances at time of divine service'. Conney was found guilty and 'ordered to confess in church in the usual penitential garb'.

Morris dancing may have originated as a type of Moorish dance (hence the name), brought from Spain in the time of Edward III, but in England it was closely connected with Robin Hood plays, which became very popular in the late 15th and early 16th centuries. Performances of these plays would begin on May Day, when four young unmarried men would be appointed as Robin Hood, Friar Tuck, Little John, and Maid Marian, and there would be displays of archery and morris dancing by Robin Hood's followers, the dancers representing characters from the plays. Although there are no specific references to these plays in Herefordshire it seems likely, given all the morris dancing, that they were performed. As 'Old Meg of Herefordshire' wrote in praising morris dancing in the county, 'never had Robin Hood a more deft Maid Marian'.

Robin Hood plays were often organized as a means of raising funds for the parish. In Kingston-upon-Thames people were invited to buy badges, at a penny each, which would symbolically enroll them as members of Robin Hood's gang. The plays were highly popular, and in the early 16th century the young Henry VIII cultivated his image as a man of the people by taking part in them. But as time went on the authorities became alarmed by their subversive nature, and from the middle of the century they were gradually suppressed.

Mumming plays were performed at Christmastide. They were transmitted orally from one generation to the next, gradually gaining new characters over time, and were effectively frozen only when they were finally transcribed. One example of a Herefordshire mumming play is known, written down by an inhabitant of Ross in 1908; it features St. George, introduced to the audience by his father the King of Egypt. St. George kills a mysterious cast of characters, their significance long since lost, including Prince Valentine, Captain Rover, Turkey Snipe (a corruption of 'Turkish Knight', as this character is called in other plays), Little John, Bonaparte, and Sambo. A doctor then revives all of St. George's victims, before killing St. George himself. Finally, at the end of most mumming plays, St. George would be revived, his return to life symbolising resurrection, the annual death of the year and its renewal in spring. Other characters who play walk-on parts are Beelzebub, Farmer Toddy, Head Per Nip, and Dicky Hissum. It begins with a short prologue;

> Ladies and Gentlmen all, if you wish to see
> We are come this night to act a royal comedy
> We are but actors young —
> We never acted before —
> But we'll do the best we can,
> And the best can do no more.
> If you don't believe what I say, —
> Walk in, old Father Christmas, and boldly lead the way.

Enter Father Christmas with besom

> Then in comes I old Father Christmas:
> Christmas or Christmas not,
> I hope old Father Christmas
> 'll never be forgot.
> For when he does appear
> It's like the rising sun in three score year.
> Room, room, galliant room! Give me room to reign.
> Your activity, my activity, such activities you never saw before.
> 'Tis I that leads the King of Egypt up to the door.

Exit Father Christmas and enter King of Egypt

> In comes I the King of Egypt, who plainly doth appear,
> Likewise St. George, my only son and heir.

Walk in St. George and act thy part
That all the people in this house
May see thy wondrous works with all their heart.

Enter St. George

Then in comes I St. George who did from England spring,
Oft-times do my wondrous works do four-fold to begin.
Girt in a closet I was kept
And then upon a cabin set,
And then upon a rock of stone,
When Satan made my body moan;
I slew the fiery dragon; I beat him to a slaughter,
And by those means I won the King of Egypt's daughter.
I fought him off most manfully,
But still came on the victory
Where is man that will against me stand?
I will cut him down with my courage in hand.

Enter Prince Valentine

In comes I Prince Valentine; if there's anyone so old,
That will give to me his lofty courage bold,
If his blood's hot, I will soon fetch it cold.

St. George and Prince Valentine fight. St. George kills him

As a final footnote, it is interesting to note plays apparently performed by the large and wealthy Jewish community in medieval Hereford. In 1286 Bishop Richard Swinfield excommunicated a number of citizens m Hereford for attending an elaborate Jewish wedding in the city, at which a play of some sort had been performed.

Chapter II
Noblemen's Players

At the same time as obliterating the old religious and folk drama, the authorities in the 1570s also tightened the laws regulating strolling players, who had first appeared a century before. Now players had to be 'servants of any Baron of this Realm', or 'any other honourable personage of greater degree'; players without such patrons were categorised as rogues and vagabonds.

In 1572 the players of the Earl of Leicester were the first to receive permission to perform, on condition that their plays were first submitted to the Master of the Revels for approval. The following decades saw a burgeoning of companies of players under either royal or noble patronage. In 1583 the first royal company was formed, and soon most great households had their own players, who, when not required by their masters, were given permission to tour the country, performing the plays of Marlowe, Shakespeare, Johnson, Webster and other contemporary playwrights. By the late 16th century most country towns could expect at least an occasional visit by one or other of these troupes of travelling players. They would as a rule have numbered perhaps eight or ten men, their chief actors riding on horseback, with their costumes and props carried in wagons.

There are references to various interlude players in Hereford in 1577, and the city received a visit from the Prince's Men in 1609; there might also have been a visit by Lord Strange's Men in the 1590s. Hereford had many more visits—the city was said to be receptive to drama—but the surviving records only list frequent blanket payments 'to the players' between 1577 and 1627. Leominster was visited, between 1596 and 1603, and again between 1613 and 1620, by a whole series of travelling players, whose tours would very probably have included Hereford as well. Whereas in Leominster the players were paid by the city authorities (the equivalent records for Hereford no longer exist), the one company we know to have visited Hereford, the Prince's Men, was paid by the Cordwainers. The surviving chancellor's accounts for Leominster record each of the players' visits, and how much each company was paid—the payments presumably reflecting either the status of the players or the number of actors:

Medieval dancers

1596-97	the Queen's Majesty's players	paid 20s.
1597-98	the Earl of Derby's players	10s.
	Lord Chandos's players	6s. 8d.
1599-1600	Lord Stafford's players	6s. 8d.
1600-01	the Queen's players	20s
	the Earl of Worcester's players	10s.
	Lord Berkeley's players	10s.
	Lord Dudley's players	6s.
1602-03	the Earl of Huntingdon's players	6s. 8d.
1613-14	Lady Elizabeth's players	5s.
1616-17	the Earl of Derby's players	5s.
	Lady Elizabeth's players	10s.
	the Earl of Sussex's players	5s.
	the Prince's players	10s.
	the Queen's Highness's players	10s.
1618-19	the Queen's players	7s.
1619-20	the Earl of Derby's players	6s. 8d.
	Lady Elizabeth's players	10s.
	players of the Towne by Mr. Baylief his appoyntment	20s.
	the King of Bohemia's players	10s.

The Earl of Worcester's players, who came to Leominster in 1600-01, had been one of the most prestigious companies back in the 1580s; on the accession of James I in 1603 they were appointed as the players of the new queen, Anne of Denmark, and in 1602, as the Queen's players, began acting in the Rose Theatre in London, specialising in domestic comedy, history and adventure plays. By 1612 the company had three branches: a London company and two separate provincial companies, one under Martin Slater, the other under Thomas Swinnerton; and it was one or other of these (or even both on separate occasions) which came to Leominster twice in 1616-19 as the Queen's players, or Queen's Highness's players.

The King of Bohemia's players, who visited Leominster in 1619-20, were originally formed in the 1580s as the Admiral's Men, under the patronage of Lord Howard of Effingham, hero of the Armada. At that date the leading company in England, the Admiral's Men included the great tragic actor Edward Alleyn. On the accession of James I in 1601 the Admiral's Men obtained the patronage of the heir to the throne, Prince Henry, and as the Prince's Men visited Hereford in 1609. When Prince Henry died prematurely in 1612 the role of patron was taken over by Frederick V, the Elector Palatine, then betrothed to the king's daughter, the Lady Elizabeth. In 1619 Frederick became King of Bohemia for one year, before being defeated in battle by catholic forces; and for this one year, therefore, the Prince's Men became the King of Bohemia's players. Lady Elizabeth herself gave her name in 1611 to another company which was beginning to make a mark at court after playing largely in the provinces, and in the following years her players came to Leominster twice. It is interesting too to note the 'players of the Towne', who were paid the large sum of 20s., presumably reflecting the size of the company.

Where the travelling players' performances took place in Hereford and Leominster is a matter of conjecture. In Gloucester the 'Bothall' was used for plays, and Hereford's Booth Hall, bought by the city in 1392, could have served the same purpose. Other performances would probably have taken place in inn yards. F.C. Morgan, former city librarian, noted an old story that in Elizabethan times a theatre had existed in Aubrey Street in Hereford; if so, this would

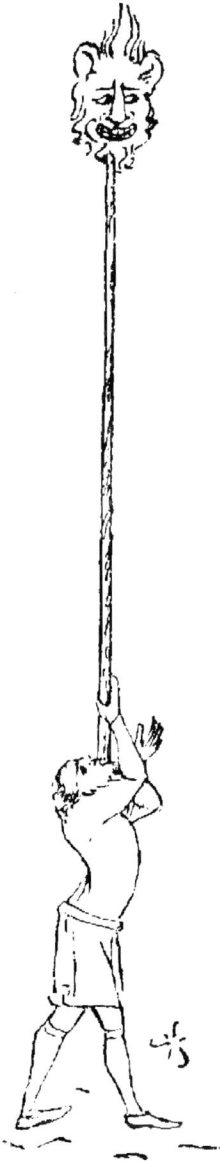

14th-century juggler

11

have been not a purpose-built theatre but an inn yard used by travelling players. There are no records, though, of any inns in Aubrey Street large enough to have had suitable yards. We have little idea of the nature of the audiences in Herefordshire, but other provincial theatres attracted people from many miles around.

The death of James I in 1625 heralded the end of noblemen's troupes of players. With the rising tide of puritanism most drama disappeared. In 1642 stage plays were banned, and theatres pulled down. In 1648 an edict was published stating that stage plays were not to be tolerated among those who professed the Christian religion.

CHAPTER III
From Nell Gwyn to David Garrick

After the Restoration the puritan ban on stage plays was lifted. Theatres reappeared, but in a form tightly controlled by the monarchy. In 1662 Charles II gave patents to two playwrights, Thomas Killigrew and Sir William Davenant, the patents specifying that women's parts might now be played by women.

Nell Gwyn (1650-87) was one of this first generation of actresses, and certainly the most celebrated. Her birthplace is uncertain, but there is a long-standing tradition that she was born in Hereford, in a house in Pipe Well Lane, later renamed Gwynne Street. Her grandfather, who is said to have come from Hereford, was a churchman who became a canon of Christ Church in Oxford. Her father was an army captain, who probably fought on the Royalist side in the Civil War and left Oxford on the Royalist defeat. He returned—the story goes—to his father's home town of Hereford, where he became a brewer, and it was here that his daughter Nell was born. She and her sister went to live in London—in Covent Garden—with their mother, both sisters being put to work selling fruit and vegetables from barrows, or possibly serving drinks in a brothel. In 1671 the mother was apparently drowned in the Thames while intoxicated. Meanwhile Nell, with a gift for mimicry and repartee, was chosen to sell oranges—the 17th-century equivalent of ice cream or popcorn—at the Theatre Royal, Drury Lane, under the management of Thomas Killigrew.

Nell Gwyn must have been a very attractive girl, with exquisite legs, a dainty figure, and beautiful reddish-brown hair. Her infectious high spirits, combined with recklessness, generosity, and a ready wit, appealed to a generation reacting to the rigours of puritanism with a determination to enjoy themselves. Selling oranges in the pit, she would have mixed with a relatively smart set of people. Killigrew recognised her talent, and she was probably brought into the company as a trainee. She first appeared on stage in 1665, at the age of 15, playing the role of

Cydaria in Dryden's *The Indian Emperor*. This role did not suit her, but Dryden provided her instead with a succession of parts written for her and more in keeping with her lively personality.

Samuel Pepys was highly taken with Nell Gwyn. They first met at a performance in 1667 of *Mustapha* by the Earl of Orrery, when he 'sat next to pretty, witty Nell at the King's House, which pleased me mightily'. In the same year, 1667, Nell achieved her greatest success, playing the 'breeches part' of the seductive Florimell in Dryden's *Secret Love*. Pepys, greatly impressed by both the play and the heroine, saw the play a dozen or more times. He wrote that 'it is one of his [Dryden's] finest comedies, and contains the best part Nell ever played – so great a performance of a comic part was never I believe in the world before – and so done by Nell, her merry part as cannot be better done in nature'. Successful and popular, she was given more and more prominent roles in the company's repertoire.

The building reputed to be Nell Gwyn's birth-place in Hereford, as in a photograph of c.1869

Nell Gwyn came to the attention of Charles II in 1667, in the following manner, as related in the *Monthly Review* for 1800:

> At the Duke's theatre, under Killigrew's patent, the celebrated Nokes appeared in a hat larger than usually assigned to Pistol, which diverted the audience so much as to help off a bad play. Dryden, in return, caused a hat to be made of the circumference of a large coach-wheel, and made Mrs. Gwynne speak an epilogue under the umbrella of it, with the brim stretched out in its utmost horizontal extension, not unlike a mushroom of that size. No sooner did she appear in this strange dress, than the house was in convulsions of laughter. Amongst the rest, the king gave the fullest proofs of appro-

bation, by going behind the scenes after the play, and taking her home in his coach to sup with him. After this elevation she still continued on the stage, and shewed great powers in exhibiting the airy, fantastic, and sprightly effusions of the comic muse.

Nell remained at Drury Lane until 1670, with intervals when all London theatres were closed in 1665 because of the plague, and in 1667 when, as the mistress of Lord Buckhurst, she briefly went to live in Epsom. In her last appearance on stage, in 1670, she played the part of Almahide in Dryden's *The Conquest of Grenada*, but the opening had to be postponed for several months awaiting her return to the stage after the birth of her first son by the king, who was born in apartments in Lincoln's Inn Fields on 8 May 1670. The baby was named Charles Beauclerk, and given the titles of Baron Headington and Earl of Burford. Later, in 1684, he was created Duke of St. Albans.

Because of her lowly origins Nell Gwyn was not thought worthy of a title, unlike her rivals in the king's heart Louise de Querouaille, given the title of Duchess of Portsmouth, and the Countess of Castlemaine, given the title of Duchess of Cleveland, but as some compensation the king gave her the freehold of a house in Pall Mall. As the king's favourite mistress she became an important political hostess, at the centre of public affairs, and the friend of wits, courtiers, and statesmen. Tradition has it that she persuaded the king to set up the Chelsea Hospital, the uniforms of its pensioners modelled on those of the Coningsby Hospital in Hereford.

Nell Gwyn's second son by the king was born on Christmas Day 1671, but died in 1680. Her grandson, James Beauclerk, was later to become Bishop of Hereford,

Charles and II and Nell Gwyn by Edward Ward
(Victoria & Albert Museum& Bridgeman Art Library)

but Nell Gwyn is unlikely to have visited Hereford as an adult. After King Charles's death, in accordance with his reported last words—'Let not poor Nelly starve'—King James II helped Nell financially. She bought an estate in Nottinghamshire, and seems to have spent her last years in comfort.

In the early 18th century theatres still existed under sufferance, subject to the licencing system introduced after the Restoration in 1660. An Act of 1713 included 'common players of interludes' in the category of rogues and vagabonds. In 1737 Walpole, exasperated by the lampooning of his cabinet on stage, passed a Licencing Act, forbidding the setting up of unauthorised playhouses. Only two, which had royal patents, were permitted to remain open—Covent Garden, and the Theatre Royal, Drury Lane. Under the new Act, all players had to have official approval in the form of either letters patent from the king, or a licence from the Lord Chamberlain. Anyone acting for reward without a licence now fell into the category of rogues and vagabonds.

As the century progressed, the status of the theatre was transformed. Acting, regarded early in the century as a somewhat disreputable activity, barely tolerated by the law, became by its end not just accepted, but the very height of fashion. One of the major causes of this transformation, and one of the most influential figures in the history of theatre in England, was the Herefordian—by birth at least—David Garrick. Born at the Angel Inn on the corner of Widemarsh Street and Maylord Street, Garrick was baptised at All Saints' Church on 28 February 1717. The actor Charles Mathews, who visited Hereford in 1830, was struck by how picturesque the Angel Inn was, and remarked to the landlord: 'Altogether Mr. Garrick *ought* to have been born here'. In fact it was quite fortuitous; it so happened that Garrick's father, an army captain, had come to the city on recruiting service with his heavily pregnant wife in tow. Garrick always regarded Lichfield, where he was brought up, as his home town; his mother was the daughter of a canon of Lichfield Cathedral. His grandfather, who was of Huguenot origin, had anglicised his name from Garric to Garrick.

On finishing his schooling Garrick travelled out to Portugal, and started work for an uncle in Lisbon who was in the wine trade. However, for one reason or another this was not a success, and Garrick returned to his parents in Lichfield. Soon afterwards he travelled up to London—in the company of Dr. Johnson—and began to study law, until he gave that up in favour of a second attempt at the wine trade. When this was not a success he began to consider the idea of becoming an actor. Acting was his great enthusiasm, much to the dismay of his family, who were appalled to learn that he was even contemplating entering so low a profession. Nevertheless, in March 1741 he was given a part as an understudy at a small London theatre, and on the strength of this performance was taken on by a professional company, making his debut in Ipswich. His first performance in London, in October 1741, was in the title role in *Richard III*, at the Goodman's Fields Theatre. The sensation of Garrick's debut performance has become part of theatre history; he astonished his contemporaries in the same way that Sarah Siddons did at a later date. Garrick's style of acting seemed a revolutionary departure from the conventions of the period; it was a natural style, based on sharply observed characterisation, in contrast to the formal manner of declamation then common. London society flocked to see him; it was said that the performance drew a dozen dukes a night.

Soon afterwards Garrick joined the cast of the Theatre Royal, Drury Lane, where he stayed for some years, in 1747 becoming a joint patentee, and subsequently sole manager. In the 29 years that he was there he transformed the nature of English theatre, as well as the social status of the acting profession. He introduced new interpretations of existing plays, championing Shakespeare, whose plays had hitherto been relatively neglected. He salvaged some of Shakespeare's plays from their Restoration 'improvements', but at the same time reworked others; thus *The Taming of the Shrew* he turned into the more anodyne *Catherine and Petruchio*. He also wrote a number of farces, such as *Miss in her Teens, or the Medley of Lovers* and *Bon Ton, or High Life above Stairs*, and collaborated with Colman in writing *The Clandestine Marriage*. A highly successful showman and self-publicist, in 1769 Garrick held a Shakespeare Jubilee at Stratford, complete with a grand procession of Shakespeare's characters, which, when the original was rained off, was staged in London and deemed a major success.

Garrick's acting had huge emotional force, and he used every means possible to increase its effect. It is said that for his performance as Hamlet he had a wig-maker produce a trick wig whose hair could be made to stand on end in his confrontation with his father's ghost. As a theatre manager, he was always innovative and keen to experiment with new and elaborate styles of scenery; he also started to use lighting in a more effective way, replacing chandeliers with concealed lighting and putting candles in a box at the front of the stage. He also introduced more authentic costumes into his productions.

Many of Garrick's changes were controversial. At this date, and until well into the 19th century, performances would consist of a prologue, the main play, one or more interludes or songs, and then a farce, the evening lasting from six to ten o'clock or later. It had been the custom to allow half price admission after eight o'clock, when the main play had usually finished, but at Drury Lane Garrick tried to end this practice. He also tried to prevent members of the audience from standing at the sides of the stage, a practice that considerably annoyed the cast.

After a long affair with the Irish actress Peg Woffington, Garrick married a French dancer, Eva Maria Veigel, in 1749. A few years later, increasingly wealthy and successful, he bought a country villa near Hampton Court, and in 1763 the couple embarked on a Grand Tour, bringing back quantities of paintings and furniture. Garrick's final appearance on stage was on 10 June 1776. At Christmas 1778 his health collapsed, and he died on 20 January 1779. He was accorded a grand funeral and buried in Westminster Abbey, his pallbearers being the Duke of Devonshire, Lord Camden, Lord Ossory, Lord Spencer, and Lord Palmerston; such respectability for an actor would have seemed extraordinary a few decades earlier. In addition he left £100,000—at that time a huge fortune.

By the 1770s theatre-going had reached the very height of fashion, with amateur theatricals highly popular among the gentry, their performances often stiffened by a backbone of professionals. At the same time many performances by professional actors advertised the appearance of a 'distinguished amateur' or a 'lady' or 'gentleman', or often 'a gentleman, his first appearance on this or any stage'. At the same time some country houses, such as Stoke Edith, east of Hereford, even boasted their own theatres. The new modishness of the theatre was demonstrated by a new magazine which appeared in 1772, entitled *The Macaroni and Theatrical Magazine* (a macaroni, in the 18th century, was a dandified figure who aped foreign fashions) with articles on famous actors and satirical pieces on, for example, 'how far players do or do not come under the description of Vagabonds'. Finally, with the Sixty Day Act in 1788, the law caught up with the times; this Act permitted the performance of plays in a given place for up to 60 days, provided the manager obtained a licence from the local magistrate. The *Hereford Journal* welcomed 'the emancipation of country theatres from a very rigid, impolitic law'. With this new freedom came a rush of theatre building, funded by generous subscriptions from the well-to-do. A theatre was a visible proof of the prestige of a town at a time when a knowledge of the finer points of acting was an essential social accomplishment.

CHAPTER IV
Strolling Players

Itinerant, or 'strolling' players, of varying degrees of respectability, had existed as early as the 1480s, when some of them were fortunate enough to obtain noble patronage. They re-emerged after the Civil War, when the age of noblemen's players had passed. By the early 1700s, groups of strollers could often be found at fairs, markets and other places likely to provide good audiences. They would travel from town to town, usually on foot, with their scenery and props carried with them in carts. In theory at least, they would carry with them a licence from the Lord Chamberlain. They performed in makeshift theatres in inn yards, barns—hence 'barn-storming'—or sometimes, if they were particularly favoured by the authorities, in town halls or guildhalls.

Traditionally they would advertise their performances to the ceremonial beating of a drum, with one member of the troupe announcing the evening's entertainment while other actors handed out playbills. Most importantly, they had to solicit the favour of the local gentry on whose patronage they depended, and they would carry letters of recommendation from one squire to another. They depended too on the goodwill of the local magistrates. Though in time actors were tolerated in the provinces, and a reputable company would encounter little difficulty, any magistrate could if he wished invoke the Licensing Act to fine actors; the informer would receive half the fine and the parish poor the other half. If the offending actor did not pay up he could be jailed for up to six months. It was therefore all-important to stay on good terms with the authorities, and as soon as a company of players arrived in a town the manager would visit the magistrate, who usually gave permission (illegally) provided that the takings from a stipulated number of nights were given to a suitable charitable cause. Thus one of Roger Kemble's performances in Hereford, in 1769, was 'for the benefit of the Widows of the Weaver's Hospital in

Hereford'. To evade the law forbidding all acting for reward without a licence, performances were routinely advertised as 'concerts of music', in which the players charged for the musical entertainment and performed a play, *gratis*, in the interval. A variation of this was to charge for tea while giving a free perfomance.

By the mid 18th century, with improved roads, theatres outside London had coalesced into a series of 'circuits' containing perhaps 10 or 15 theatres, most of which would receive a visit perhaps annually, or at least once every three years or so. The most important theatres outside London were in Dublin, Edinburgh, and Bath (which secured a royal patent in 1768, after a lengthy campaign). A handful of other provincial theatres, such as the York Theatre, also had high reputations; York was on the northern circuit, run by Tate Wilkinson, one of the better provincial managers.

The strolling players would if possible time their visits to coincide with the Assizes, the race meetings or the fairs. Towns likely to provide a good audience would have to be of a reasonable size, and with families of rank and fortune living in the neighbourhood; it was said that a strolling company was most likely to be successful in a town where above 40 gentlemen's coaches were kept.

Until the late 18th century most strolling companies would practice a 'sharing' system, where any profits would be divided equally after the deduction of expenses; the manager, though, would take three or four extra shares as payment for providing the costumes and scenery. Since a large part of the cast would consist of members of his family, the manager would in practice take the lion's share of the profits. Later on it became more usual for the manager to pay his actors a wage. Recruitment was haphazard. Some actors were recruited through the 'houses of call', taverns in Covent Garden frequented by actors in search of employment. They had to be able to play all the stock roles; even better if they could sing, recite poetry and dance the hornpipe as well. They would be recruited for a 'line' of parts; in other words, a tragic actor would be expected to play a number of defined tragic parts—Lear, Macbeth, and so on—and a comic actor to play all the stock comic parts. A manager would also enquire how many lines an actor could learn in an evening—in most theatres the programme changed nightly, and consequently large numbers of plays had to be memorised.

Most actors started in the provinces, graduating to the London theatres if they were good, and even those who achieved eminence in later life, such as John Philip Kemble, had to endure extremes of penury in their early days, as the following story shows:

One night when he [Kemble] was to appear as Ventidius in *All for Love*, he was much embarrassed by his landlady retaining his shirt, which she had to wash, until he paid fifteen pence which was due, but which it was impossible, in this emergency, to raise. The rest of the company were in equal distress; and to add to the want of a shirt, only one ruffle could be found among them. To elude the observations of the audience, Ventidius was therefore obliged to manoeuvre, and he pinned the single ruffle on his right hand, and went through the whole of the first act with his left hand wrapped up in his cloak; but naturally supposing that the audience would consider it strange that he should only use his right hand, he kept occasionally shifting the ruffle from one hand to the other, and thus evaded observation.

The groups of strollers varied from the eminently respectable to the downright disreputable. The former category included John Ward's players, taken over on his retirement by Roger Kemble and in turn, on Kemble's retirement, by John Boles Watson, builder of the Hereford Theatre. At the other extreme was the Waldegrave Company of Comedians, whose manager Charles Waldegrave was reputed to be fond of assaulting men as they came from the tavern, while his wife was said to be in the habit of prostituting her actresses in the hope of acquiring influence in the towns where they played.

Given this record, it is not really surprising that the theatre had a lot of enemies. Garrick may have improved the reputation of the acting profession, but the immorality and scandalous conduct of the more disreputable strollers offended many, as did the lasciviousness of Restoration drama. Evangelical churchmen were particularly vehement in their denunciations of the stage, and the eventual closure of the Hereford Theatre in 1857 was said to be partially due to the hostility of the clergy in the city. Because many strollers were little more than thieves and trick-

Roger Kemble by Humphrey

sters, even the more reputable companies were likely to be treated with suspicion.

This was the fate that befell Thomas Mildenhall, who had been performing in Hereford in John Crisp's company. In 1829 Mildenhall, who was also a play-wright and scene painter, decided to set up his own company to perform his plays, including *The Man of Ross*, a dramatisation he had written of the life of John Kyrle. He collected together a group including at least one other actor from Crisp's company, and in the summer of 1829 they set off on the road, performing in Ross, Ledbury, Monmouth, Chepstow and South Wales. In Ledbury and Monmouth they were very successful, the neigh-bouring gentry flocking to see them. In Ross, however, they were treated

David Garrick
by an unknown artist

with suspicion because of the scandalous behaviour of some previous strollers. In Chepstow their reception was even worse, and Mildenhall lost a considerable amount of money. Robert Dyer, Mildenhall's leading actor, explained what happened: 'We met with a most mortifying reception at Chepstow, where the miserable shifts of a set of unfortunate strollers had left such a stigma on the name of player that we were looked upon with painful suspicion. Every door was closed against us, and for the first time I felt ashamed of my profession … At last, as a special favour and then on condition that I always paid well in advance, the proprietor of a lodging house where packmen ... found harbour consented to admit us'. The offenders were probably the Davenport Company of Comedians, who are known to have visited Chepstow at about this time.

Perhaps not surprisingly, many companies of strollers lived a hand-to-mouth existence, as reflected in a contemporary satire:

'Where are my forty knights?' cries Lear.
A Page replies, 'Your Majesty, they're here.'
When lo! two bailiffs and a writ appear.
'Give me a pound of flesh,' cries Shylock, well he may
For Shylock – has not eat an ounce today!

Among the many strolling players who came to Herefordshire was Charles Macklin, who started his career wandering through Wales and the Welsh borders with one of the less reputable companies of strollers. In addition to acting, 'sometimes he was an architect and knocked up the stage and seats in a barn; sometimes he wrote an opening prologue or parting epilogue; at others he wrote a song complimentary to the village he happened to play in'. Later he accompanied a strolling band from Bath led by Lady Hawley (otherwise known as Mrs. Hayes). The Bath comedians, as they were called, seem to have been popular in Hereford and probably visited the city annually for a few years around 1730, for the Assize and Race Weeks. They played in a purpose-built booth, according to the *Gloucester Journal*, which reported in 1732 that 'notwithstanding the largeness of the booth built by the Bath comedians, they had not half room enough to hold the people'. The following year, in 1733, the Bath comedians were lucky enough to obtain four suits of rich men's clothing, and three suits of rich women's clothing, royal cast-offs sold to them by the dressmaker to the Court.

John Boles Watson

The Irish actor-manager Richard Elrington, who had first appeared as a child actor in Dublin, came to Ross in the 1740s after performing in Minchinhampton; the magistrates there had taken offence—a common hazard for strolling players—and sent him to prison for a day for offences against the Licencing Act. At about the same time, another small company in the Welsh borders was started by Charles and Mary Morison; in their 'commonwealth' any profits were shared out equally between the six members. They had previously been part of a larger strolling company, but when the manager decided to head westwards to Swansea, the six of them left to set up on their own, performing in Crickhowell, Abergavenny, Hay and other towns along the Welsh borders. Sometimes their efforts were rewarded with profits— after paying for the printing of playbills, the hire of a barn, materials for the scenery, the hiring of fiddlers and sometimes a drummer to help advertise their performance, and sundry other expenses such as candles— but often there were none. If they made a satisfactory sum of money they would share 4d. of ale between them, but if there were only modest profits they would make do with only 2d. of ale. Strolling players such as these would generally not attempt to try their luck in the major towns and cities, where the better and more reputable players were already established, and where fashionable society would not tolerate second-rate actors.

One way for a single actor to evade the clutches of the law was to become a 'lecturer', the so-called lectures consisting of anything from recitation to ventriloquism, acting or juggling. One such 'lecturer' who may have come to Herefordshire was a man known as Le Sieur Rea. An Irishman with a thick brogue, Le Sieur Rea had adopted his French name for business purposes. In 1773 he toured South Wales as a conjurer and lecturer, performing his 'Grand Medley'; after performing at Hay, he went on to Monmouth, then to Micheldean, Newnham and Chepstow. 'He possessed', wrote a disapproving contemporary, 'the impudence of the lowest of his craft without the least knowledge of it'.

The temporary theatres used by strollers such as these were often far from satisfactory, ridiculed by the sophisticated for their primitive and makeshift nature. In addition they were often located in the most unsuitable spots. In 1789 the *Hereford Journal* published a satirical poem poking fun at one (unnamed) theatre in a particularly unsuitable location:

VERSES

On a country theatre over a butcher's shambles, in this county.

Whoe'er our house examines must excuse,
The wondrous shifts of the Dramatic Muse:
Then kindly listen while the prologue rambles,
From *Wit* to *Beef* – from *Shakespeare* to the *Shambles*
    Divided only by a flight of stairs,
The Monarch swaggers, and the butcher swears;
Quick the transition, when the curtain drops,
From meak Monimia's tears to mutton chops.
While for Lothario's loss, Calista cries,
Old women scold, and dealers d–n your eyes;
Here, Juliet listens to the gentle lark;
There, in harsh chorus, hungry bull-dogs bark;

Cleavers and scimitars give blow for blow,
And heroes bleed above, and sheep below.
With weeping lovers, dying calves complain;
Confusion all – and chaos come again!
Suet and sighs, blank verse and blood abound
And form a Tragic Comedy around.
Hither your steelyards, butchers, bring to weigh
A pound of flesh – Antonio's bond to pay:
Hither your knives, ye butchers clad in blue,
Bring to be whetted by the cruel Jew.
How hard our lot, who seldom doom'd to eat,
Cast a sheep's eye at this forbidden treat;
Gaze on, sirloins, which, ah! we cannot carve,
And in the midst of legs of mutton, starve!
   But would ye to our house in crowds repair
Ye gallant captains, and ye blooming fair,
Monarchs no more would supperless remain,
Nor pregnant Queens for cutlets long in vain.

A provincial theatre performance in England, c.1788.
James Wright's engraving of Macbeth scene 1 mocks theatre outside London,
while indicating the energy of the scene and excitement of the audience

These makeshift theatres would contain a pit, a gallery, and sometimes boxes against the side and rear walls. It is difficult to be certain about just how such theatres were constructed. The stage would probably have consisted of boards supported on trestles; in one barn theatre, at least (in Essex), the gallery was improvised from a wagon suspended from the roof, with a ladder for access. Some makeshift theatres, such as those in the market houses in Ross and Ledbury, had relatively low ceilings and it is hard to see how a gallery could have been incorporated. Perhaps the 'gallery' simply referred to the seats at the back, on a raised platform. Lighting would come from candles suspended from the ceiling and dotted around the auditorium, with others in a trough at the front of the stage. In the mid-18th century oil lamps were installed at Drury Lane, but theatres in barns, such as the one shown on the engraving on the previous page, still used candles.

Chapter V
John Ward and the Kemble Family

Among the better and more reputable companies of strolling players was the Warwickshire Company of Comedians. Started by the Irish actor-manager John Ward some time before 1746, this company was, according to Ward's obituary in the *Gentleman's Magazine*, 'a respectable body of comedians'. Ward was a methodist, rather surprisingly given the contempt which most methodists had for the acting profession. The company was based in Birmingham, and its circuit stretched from Gloucester, Worcester and Stratford right up into mid-Wales, as far as Brecon and Carmarthen. Most towns in Herefordshire and the surrounding counties received at least an occasional visit once every few years. In 1748 Ward paid a visit to Hereford and put on a play at the Swan and Falcon, in Broad Street. The announcement in the *Gloucester Journal* read: 'By the Warwickshire Company of Comedians, at the Swan and Falcon in Hereford, on Monday evening being the 26th December will be acted a comedy, called: *A Bold Stroke for a Wife, or the Quaker Outwitted*. To which will be added a pantomime entertainment, called *Harlequin's Nuptials*. To begin exactly at 6 o'clock'.

Ward's company was about a dozen strong, including, from 1752, Roger Kemble, later to take over as manager. A native of Hereford, Kemble was born in 1721 in Capuchin Lane, or Church Street, where his father (thought to be a relation of the catholic priest John Kemble, executed on Widemarsh Common in 1679) was a barber. Roger followed his father's profession and was also a wig-maker; the Hereford Record Office holds a receipt signed by him for two periwigs which he supplied to a local family, the Monningtons.

At the age of 30, a visit to a theatre in Canterbury is said to have fired Roger Kemble with enthusiasm for the stage, and in 1752 he joined John Ward's company, forsaking his safe job for a much more precarious and socially disreputable one. He was by all accounts a courteous, handsome and gentle man, and soon after joining the company he attracted the admiration of John Ward's daughter, Sally. Ward had forbidden his daughter to marry an actor, but Sally was determined to have her own way, and he finally gave his consent, reputedly saying, 'Well, my dear child, you have not disobeyed me; the devil himself could not make an actor of your husband'. (According to other accounts it was Roger himself who said these words to his own daughter, Sarah, when she insisted on marrying William Siddons, a rather indifferent actor in the Kemble Company of Players). Roger Kemble's wife, Sally, was a strong-minded woman who ruled her household with iron discipline.

Roger Kemble in later life

In addition to Hereford, John Ward's company visited Leominster, Kington, Ross, Ledbury and Bromyard. In 1752 the company visited Ledbury, where their performance of *Henry VIII* was well patronised by the gentry; from Ledbury they proceeded to Bromyard and then to Leominster. In Leominster they performed in the Schoolhouse in Church Street (formerly the Forbury Chapel, and also used as a courthouse) and returned for a 12-week season in 1757, with further visits in 1761 and 1765. At the end of their 1765 season there, Roger Kemble had a benefit performance. Benefits, where the proceeds would go to one of the actors in the company, after the deduction of expenses, were usually an actor's chief source of income, and most actors could expect to have one or two of them each year. This benefit in Leominster netted Roger Kemble £22. Tickets would usually cost 2s. for the pit and 1s. for the gallery, and although estimating the size of 18th-century theatres involves a good deal of guesswork, this Leominster theatre might have held something in the order of 200 people. A glance at the plays Ward performed in Leominster shows a varied selection of tragedies, comedies, some topical plays, and a good deal of spectacle: Shakespeare, *The Beggar's Opera, The Fair Quaker of Deal, Harlequin's Escape into a Quart Bottle*, and *The Procession of Their Majesties' Coronation*. In 1758 the company visited Kington for an

11-week season—here the theatre was in a barn, since demolished, behind the Sun Inn—and Presteigne for a short season of four weeks. In 1760 they visited Hay for five weeks, in 1761 Ross for three weeks, in 1764 Ledbury for eight weeks, and in 1766 Bromyard.

In 1761 John Ward visited Hereford again, this time for a season of 13 weeks, and probably performed in the Swan and Falcon in Broad Street, later replaced by the City Arms. He returned to Hereford in 1764, for 25 weeks; and this time Roger Kemble's benefit netted him £35, indicating that this theatre was about half as large again as the theatre in Leominster. Another actor in the company, Mr. Burden, was also given a benefit in Hereford, but ran away with his takings without paying the charges. Even in the Warwickshire Company of Comedians, not everyone was honest.

Ward retired in the mid-1760s and settled in Leominster, where he was buried on his death in 1773, his tombstone granting him the distinction of 'gentleman'. His circuit was inherited by Roger Kemble, and the company now became known as the Kemble Company of Players. They continued to visit many of the towns on Ward's circuit, but Ledbury, Ross and Bromyard seem to have been dropped. The core of the company, as with most companies of strolling players, consisted of members of the family, with Roger Kemble on stage along with his wife,

John Ward's tomb, and that of his wife Sarah, outside Leominster Priory Church.
The wording reads:
'And hopeing thro' his merits hence to rise
In glorious mode, in this dark closet lies
John Ward Gent.
Who died Oct. 30. 1773,
Aged 69.
Also, Sarah his wife, who died
Jan. 30. 1786. Aged 75 years.'

sundry children and any relations who could be mustered. Kemble seems to have been relatively well off, his 'shares' amounting to £350.

Roger and Sally Kemble had 12 children, of whom eight reached adulthood. Of these, four went onto the stage: Sarah, John Philip, Charles, and Stephen. The eldest child, Sarah, was born in 1755, above the Leg of Mutton in Brecon, where the company was then playing. Stephen was born in Kington in 1758 shortly after his mother, Sally, had left the stage when playing Anne Bullen (i.e. Boleyn) in a performance of *Henry VIII*. The Kemble children were pressed into service at an early age, and Sarah is said to have first appeared at the Kington theatre at the age of three. She apparently had a benefit at Hereford in 1761, when she would have been six years old. Long afterwards, an old acquaintance remembered her 'when a very young woman, standing by the side of her father's stage, and knocking a pair of snuffers against a candlestick, to imitate the sound of a windmill during the representation of some Harlequin piece'. Another story comes from Thomas Holcroft, briefly one of Roger Kemble's actors in the early 1770s:

> The company of which old Mr. Kemble was the manager was more respectable than many other companies of strolling players; but it was not in so flourishing a condition as to place the manager beyond the reach of the immediate smiles or frowns of fortune. Of this the following anecdote may be cited as an instance. A benefit had been fixed for some of the family, at which Miss Kemble, then a little girl, was to come forward in some part, as a juvenile prodigy. The taste of the audience was not, it seems, so accommodating as in the present day, and the extreme youth of the performer disposed the gallery to noise and uproar instead of admiration. Their turbulent dissatisfaction quite disconcerted the child, and she was retiring bashfully from the stage, when her mother, who was a woman of high spirit, and alarmed for the success of her little actress, came forward, and leading the child to the front of the house, made her repeat the fable of the Boys and the Frogs, which entirely turned the tide of popular opinion in her favour.

The young Sarah was sent off to school in Worcester, where at first she was looked down on by the other pupils. A fellow pupil wrote to her mother: 'I asked [Sarah] what her parents were, and what was their position, as indeed, dear Mama, you have advised me to do, to avoid the possibility of becoming intimate with an unsuitable or ungenteel acquaintance. But she answered without blush or confusion, that her father was Roger Kemble, the manager of a troupe of strolling players, who had arrived in the town travelling in a wagon. You can imagine my embarrassment, my dear Mama, at having exhorted so damaging a confession, and I thought it best to make a curtsey and return to the other young ladies who were awaiting my report'.

In February 1771 the Kemble company came to Hereford for a season, where the theatre would still have been in the Swan and Falcon in Broad Street. Sarah played Miss Sterling in *The Clandestine Marriage* (see illustration below), and Anne Bullen in a spectacular performance of *Henry VIII* featuring Anne Bullen's coronation, and the ceremony of the Champion in Westminster Hall, complete with 'the state canopy, armour, coronation robes, regalia and every other decoration proper for each procession'. The company now comprised Roger and Sally Kemble, their daughter Sarah, now aged 16, and Messrs. Jones, Downing, Morrison, Clifton, West, Mr. and Mrs. Crump, and Miss Shepherd. In his memoirs, Thomas Holcroft gives a vivid picture of George Downing, who had apparently, as a young man, masqueraded as a captain in order to elope with, and marry, a young girl who he had been led to believe, wrongly, was an heiress. Downing, according to Holcroft, 'had a large red bottle nose, with little intellect; but he was tall, looked passably when made up for the stage, and had a tolerable voice, though monotonous. To hide the redness of his nose it was his custom to powder it, but unluckily he drank brandy; the humour of it made him irritable, and in the course of a scene the powder was rubbed off. His wife stood behind the scenes with a powder puff ready, and exclaimed when he came off: "Lord! Curse it, George! How you

The laſt Night but one of performing in this Town.
For the BENEFIT of

Mr. *Morriſon* and Mr. *Clifton*.

AT the THEATRE in HEREFORD on FRIDAY next, MAY 31, will be preſented a celebrated COMEDY, call'd The

Clandeſtine Marriage.

Lord Ogleby, by Mr. JONES;
Sir John Melvile, by Mr. DOWNING:
Traverſe, by Mr. MORRISON;
And Lovewell, by Mr. CLIFTON;
Miſs Sterling, by Miſs KEMBLE;
Fanny, by Miſs SHEPHERD;
And Mrs. Heidelbergh, by Mrs. KEMBLE.
End of Act II. A SONG, by Mrs. CRUMP.
End of Act III. A SONG, by Mr. WEST.
End of Act IV. A DREAMING PROLOGUE,
By Mr. DOWNING.
At the End of the Play, An EPILOGUE, addreſſed to the
LADIES and GENTLEMEN of HEREFORD,
Wrote, and to be Spoken, by Mr. MORRISON.
To which will be added a COMEDY, of three Acts, call'd

Catherine and Petruchio:
OR, THE
TAMING OF THE SHREW.
Petruchio, by Mr. DOWNING;
Grumio, by Mr. JONES.
And Catherine, by Mrs. KEMBLE.
The Whole to conclude with

The Picture of a Playhouſe:
OR,
BUCKS HAVE AT YE ALL.
By Mr. CLIFTON.
PITT 2s. GALLERY 1s.
To begin at half an hour paſt ſix o'clock.

rub your poor nose! Come here and let me powder it. Do you think Alexander the Great had such a nose? I am sure Juliet would never have married Romeo with such a bottle-nose. Upon my word, if your nose had been so red and large when you ran away with me from the boarding school, I should have never have stepped into the same chaise with you". Mrs. Downing herself 'was addicted to drinking, exceedingly nervous, and sniffled when she spoke. She was often employed to receive the money at the stage door, and was suspected of petty embezzlements to supply herself with liquor'.

Returning to Sarah: two years later, in spite of her father's disapproval, she married William Siddons, by then an actor in her father's company who was, in the words of one contemporary, 'a damned rascally player, though seemingly a very civil fellow'. The following year, in 1774, the couple left the company to try and make their own way, Sarah soon receiving an offer of employment from Chamberlain and Crump. (Crump had been one of Roger Kemble's players, and Chamberlain was to join John Boles Watson's company. For a while, however, they ran a company of their own.) In due course, Garrick, then manager of the Theatre Royal, Drury Lane, had word of a promising young actress based in Cheltenham, and Sarah was invited up to London in 1775 to be tried out. As a 21-year-old provincial player, facing hostility from the established actresses at Drury Lane, she lacked confidence, and her debut there was disastrous. She returned to the provinces and spent a few years learning her craft, initially on the Yorkshire circuit, then at the Theatre Royal in Bath.

Meanwhile, Roger Kemble had sent his eldest son, John Philip, to the catholic college at Douai in France, planning that he should join the priesthood. But John Philip had other ideas, and abandoning his studies, he returned to England to become an actor. In the course of his early wanderings he met John Boles Watson, later to become manager of the Hereford Theatre, and the pair set out on the road together as itinerant players, with Kemble as reciter and Watson as supporting conjurer.

At one time—so the story goes—they were left penniless, and so hungry that they were reduced to breaking into a turnip field and gorging themselves on uncooked turnips. It was then that they hit upon a bold scheme to improve their finances; Kemble would pose as a methodist preacher, with Watson as his clerk. It was an age when methodist preachers routinely attracted huge audiences, so their scheme was not impractical, and Kemble's education at Douai College was at least put to some use. They decided to try their luck in Tewkesbury, and, having selected a meadow near the town as a suitable spot, Kemble stood on a hay cart and began to preach. The occasion was repeated in fictional form in *John Halifax, Gentleman.*

> He had given as his text one which the simple rustics received in all respects as coming from a higher and holier volume than Shakespeare - 'mercy is twice blessed. It blesseth him that gives and him that takes. 'Tis mightiest in the mightiest'. On that text he did dilate, gradually warming with his subject ... We had never heard such elegance ... No wonder it affected the rest of the audience. Feeble men, leaning on forks and rakes, shook their old heads sagely, as if they understood it all. And when the speaker alluded to the horrors of war – a subject which then came so bitterly home to every heart in Britain – many many women melted into sobs and tears. At last, when the orator, himself moved by the pictures he had conjured up, paused suddenly, quite exhausted, and asked for a slight contribution 'to help a deed of charity', there was a general rush towards him. 'No – no, my good people; no, I will not take from anyone more than a penny, and then only if they are quite sure that they can spare it ... Thank you, my very worthy and approved good masters, and a fair harvest to you'. He bowed them away in a dignified and graceful manner, still standing on the hay cart. His companion burst into roars of laughter, but the preacher looked grave. 'Hang me if I'll be at this trick again... but starvation is – excuse me – unpleasant, and necessity has no law. It is of vital consequence that I should reach Cheltenham tonight; and after walking twenty miles, one cannot easily walk ten more, and afterwards appear in Macbeth to an admiring audience'.

'We ourselves can well remember', said a friend, 'how joyously poor Watson would relate [the episode] and how earnestly he would attest the correctness of the story'.

Roger Kemble before long enrolled Watson into his company, but refused to allow his son to join him. After the members of the Kemble Players had apparently collected a subscription for him, to which his father contributed a parting guinea, John Philip then went to Birmingham in the hope that his sister Sarah, then acting there, could help him to find work. He finally made his debut in Wolverhampton in 1776, also with Crump and Chamberlain, and then in 1783 joined the cast of Drury Lane, of which he became manager in 1788; in 1803 he left Drury Lane, unable to bear the capriciousness of its manager, Richard Brinsley Sheridan, and instead bought a third of the Covent Garden patent.

Two other Kemble children followed Sarah and John Philip onto the stage, though neither had anything like the same success. According to Lord Oxberry, Charles Kemble was a 'tall awkward youth with what is

The Half Moon, Broad Street, Hereford, demolished in 1866,
where the Kemble Company of Players performed, 1778-86

termed a hatchet face, a figure badly proportioned, and evidently weak in his limbs. His acting was even worse than his appearance'. Charles, however, became joint manager of Covent Garden in 1817, when John Philip handed over his interests to his brother; and another brother, Stephen, had a respectable career as an actor, though not achieving the eminence of his two famous siblings.

Roger Kemble continued touring around the theatres on his circuit. Hereford received another visit in 1775, when performances were given of *Richard III, The Grecian Daughter, Comus, The Beggar's Opera,* and Garrick and Colman's *The Clandestine Marriage*. The venue for these plays was the Swan and Falcon in Broad Street. A few years later, in 1778, Kemble moved across Broad Street to the Half Moon. The *Hereford Journal* announced:

> Mr. Kemble presents his compliments to the ladies and gentlemen of the City of Hereford and its vicinity, and begs leave to inform them that he has fitted up, at great expense, an elegant Theatre in the Half Moon, Broad Street, which he intends opening this evening. He likewise begs leave to assure the public that he has collected most of his performers from Theatres Royal; and hopes they will prove ornaments to their profession, in giving entire satisfaction to their audience; which has ever been the pride and desire of their most obedient servant.

34

CHAPTER VI
John Boles Watson & the Hereford Theatre

In 1783 Kemble retired, at the age of 52, leaving the Kemble Company of Players and its circuit in the capable and businesslike hands of John Boles Watson.

Like Kemble's predecessor John Ward, Watson was an Irishman, a man of wit and charm as well as entrepreneurial ability. His family had intended him to become a merchant, but he was determined to make the theatre his career. After his early adventures as an itinerant player, tramping through the country with John Philip Kemble, followed by a few years acting in Roger Kemble's company, Watson had decided that management was more to his taste, and in 1782 he built a theatre of his own in the newly fashionable resort of Cheltenham. The new theatre was to receive the ultimate accolade a few years later, in July 1788, when King George III and his wife Queen Caroline came to Cheltenham to take the waters. The king, a keen theatregoer, was staying in the town for a few days, and was persuaded to visit the theatre one evening; he enjoyed himself so much that he and his wife made further visits. The evening before his departure he was entertained by a gala performance with a farce, *The Chapter of Accidents*, in which George Shuter, Watson's leading actor—'from the name alone the actor must be a damn droll dog!' the king is reported to have said—was playing a village dolt. The evening was voted a success, and at the end Watson composed a 'farewell address', spoken by another actor, Mr. Charlton.

Busy in Cheltenham, Gloucester, and the surrounding towns from July to September, during the rest of the year Watson and his company, now proudly calling themselves Their Majesties' Servants, visited the other theatres on the circuit—in Herefordshire, the Midlands, and up into Wales—usually visiting each of its theatres at least once every three years.

In 1783 Watson decided to build a theatre in Hereford to replace Roger Kemble's temporary theatre fitted up in the Half Moon in Broad

Street. In September 1785 he bought a plot of land adjoining the Half Moon, on its south side (the site of the theatre is now occupied by Kemble House), and stretching from Broad Street down to Wroughtall Street (now Aubrey Street). The plot of land was a garden belonging to Isaac Skyrme, whose property adjoined it on the south side, and Watson paid Skyrme £100 for it. As his builder Watson employed William Parker, described as a joiner and cabinet maker but also very active as a builder in the city. Parker built an attractive but small theatre, 76ft. 6in. long and 35ft. wide, with a carriageway beside it on the south side, with harness room above, and a yard and stables to the rear. Its façade would probably have been fairly plain, except for a pediment ornamented with busts of Shakespeare, Garrick and Powell, and there was a dome of some sort(at least this was the case in 1816). As payment Parker was to take half the proceeds of three benefit performances each season, known as 'the Builder's Nights'.

William Powell, whose bust was put in such illustrious company, was a Herefordian who had risen to fame as an actor in Garrick's company. Born in Hereford in 1735, and educated at Hereford Grammar School and Christ's Hospital, he started work in London as clerk to a distiller, but after becoming involved with amateur theatricals was introduced to Garrick in 1758 as a young actor of promise. Highly impressed, Garrick offered Powell an immediate engagement at Drury Lane. Horace

Arrangement of PLAYS this Week, &c.
By their MAJESTIES SERVANTS,

From the THEATRE-ROYAL, CHELTENHAM.
THEATRE, HEREFORD.

ON THURSDAY (for the 9th Subscription-night) O'KEEFFE's two moſt favourite Pieces, acted at the Haymarket and Covent-garden, above 300 nights within theſe five ſeaſons laſt paſt.—The Dreſſes, Scenery, and Decorations, by the beſt artiſts, and the very ſame as in London, viz.
To-morrow the 6th inſt. (to begin exactly at SIX o'clock)
THE YOUNG QUAKER,
A COMEDY in Five Acts.
With (a Sequel to The POOR SOLDIER—)
PATRICK IN PRUSSIA;
Or, LOVE IN A CAMP.
The MUSIC adapted, compiled, and partly compoſed by Mr. SHIELD.
☞ SUCH THINGS ARE, and INKLE AND YARICO, having been already performed, cannot be repeated in the ſubſcription; but, by deſire of ſeveral ladies and gentlemen, theſe two favorite Pieces will be preſented together, on SATURDAY, for the laſt time poſitively that either will be acted this ſeaſon.
††† On MONDAY (the 10th ſubſcription-night) Mr. BLAND will make his firſt appearance—the Play, The SUSPICIOUS HUSBAND, and the New Farce, called The FIRST FLOOR.
⁎ Allan Ramſay's SCOTS PASTORAL (never acted here) called The GENTLE SHEPHERD, will be performed next week, newly compoſed by T. LINLEY, Eſq. and The PILGRIM, written by Beaumont and Fletcher (latterly revived by John Kemble, Eſq. Manager of Drury-lane Theatre), is getting ready.——Of the performance of all the capital New Pieces, notice will be regularly given in his Paper.

Newspaper advertisement for 6 November 1788

Walpole noted: 'There is come forth within these ten days a young actor, who has turned the heads of the whole town. The first night of his appearance the audience, not content with clapping, stood up and shouted'. Powell made his debut in Beaumont and Fletcher's *Philaster*, though he was apparently 'so very much frightened he could not speak for some time, and when he did the tears ran fast down his cheeks – but he soon recovered himself, and went through the part with a great deal of nature and feeling'.

Powell became a partner in a new theatre in Bath which opened in May 1766. In July 1769, however, while staying in Bristol, he rashly stripped off his shirt after playing in a cricket match, and threw himself down on a patch of damp grass. As a result he developed pneumonia, and died a month later, aged only 34.

The new theatre in Hereford, complete with its busts, opened in September 1786, a year after Watson's purchase of the site; the *Hereford Journal* reported that 'Mr. Watson has kept his word in building a very handsome theatre for the accommodation of this city, and there is every reason to think that he will introduce performers and apparatus that will do credit to it; his company having met with astonishing applause this summer in Cheltenham, and the splendour of the scenery and dresses thought equal to any in the kingdom'.

Inside, the theatre consisted of a gallery (price 2s.), and a pit (price 1s.), and provided £40 takings per night, or up to £60 on popular benefit nights. The size of the takings provides a rough measure of the capacity, and, though it is difficult to be certain, the Hereford Theatre might have seated five or six hundred, rich and poor alike all sitting on wooden benches. The gallery would have run round three sides of the auditorium, its panels probably painted sea-green and decorated with painted swags. The main part of the gallery would have had room for perhaps half a dozen rows of benches rising on a raked floor, the side galleries, two benches wide, running along the walls to meet the proscenium. Later, boxes were installed, and these would have run round three sides of the auditorium below the gallery. Lighting came from oil lamps rather than candles, with several hanging above the proscenium, some in the wings, and further lamps in a movable trough at the front of the stage. The auditorium remained lit all through the evening, except in special circumstances—for example for a Phantasmagoria. Heating came from fires in the auditorium—and in the summer from the steamy conviviality of the audience.

The stage of a Georgian theatre was in two sections: the acting and the scenic areas. Nearest to the audience was an apron, the proscenium, jutting out into the house. This was flanked on either side by proscenium doors. Until about 1790 most action took place on the proscenium, with the proscenium arch behind and the scenery set in grooves in the main part of the stage. The cloth curtain covering the proscenium opening was always a deep olive colour. In front of the stage was the orchestra pit containing a small orchestra, which in 1824 included a violin, a flute, and a pedal harp.

Contemporary theatres were far from comfortable. The leg-room in the side galleries was usually constricted, and the visibility in them so poor that those in the second row had to stand up in order to see properly. It had been common practice for members of the audience to stand at the sides of the stage, but this was an extreme inconvenience for the actors, and Watson, like Garrick, repeatedly tried to stop the practice. He also had to try to dissuade members of the audience from going behind the scenes during the performance. At one stage, in 1793, the situation must have become completely out of hand, because Watson was reduced to pleading in the *Hereford Journal* with his audiences to stay in the auditorium: 'experience proves that the Theatre holds with ease BEFORE the curtain many more Pounds than has been the receipts on particular Benefits where the scenes have been crouded [*sic*]; and the Performances rendered disgusting and every way unpleasant. To do justice therefore to the audience no Person whatever shall again be admitted behind the scenes (but those professionally concerned) on any of the Stock Nights or Performers' Benefits'. It was a persistent problem, however, and the plea had to repeated time and time again.

In the absence of boxes (which were not installed until 1798, in time for Sarah Siddons's appearance in August of that year), the more affluent members of society—landed gentry, members of masonic orders, the 'gallant captains', and the 'blooming fair'—would have sat on the benches in the pit, together with tradesmen, lawyers and suchlike. The gallery, with its cheaper seats, would have attracted a rowdy audience of apprentices, farm workers and ordinary soldiers; in the 1820s, at least, they were not above throwing projectiles at the unfortunate people below.

Audiences were not just passive spectators, they could be noisy and rude, and actors who had incurred their disapproval would frequently find themselves hissed and pelted with oranges and apples. On one occasion in the Shrewsbury Theatre in the 1830s, as told in Robert Dyer's *Nine Years of an Actor's Life*, the eminent actor William Charles Macready was performing in his benefit, and in the audience were a proverbially noisy group of Shrewsbury butchers. 'The noise was so intense, and the confusion so terrific that Macready stopped and said, "Ladies and

A late Georgian audience. From a print by Cruickshank

Gentlemen, I have played William Tell many, many times, but indeed the frightful noise you make entirely drives the recollection of the words from me". An awful silence ensued for a moment, when a bull-like voice shouted from the gallery: "Why, you have a good house, you ———, so go on, go on!" and he did go on, though he appeared annihilated by the rude command'.

Londoners tended to regard provincial audiences as hopelessly unsophisticated and uncultured. On the whole this was probably unjust, though some theatres had very poor reputations. Leeds, for example, was known as the Botany Bay of actors. There are many stories concerning the naiviety of provincial audiences, such as another recounted by Robert Dyer: 'In country theatres comic incidents will sometimes occur in the most tragic scenes, through the innocent simplicity of the audience. On one occasion, we played *Lovers' Vows*, and when Frederick enquired "Is there a doctor in the village?", a matter-of-fact countryman replied in a tone of sympathy, "Oh yes sir, there's Old Parfit, the horse-doctor, lives up in town"'.

In the 18th century many performances, known as 'bespeaks', were advertised as being 'by special request of' or 'by desire of' a patron—the

usual formula was 'by desire and under the immediate patronage of'—
who either guaranteed a certain sum of money or bought a proportion
of the better seats for distribution among friends, thereby gaining the
privilege of choosing the entertainment for the evening. Not surprisingly
it was the more popular plays that were bespoken in this way. Some
patrons were army officers, others were clubs or societies, groups of
gentlemen or, increasingly after the turn of the century, individuals. A
look at the patrons who bespoke performances at the theatre provides a
fascinating snapshot of theatregoing—or rather theatre-patronising—
society in Hereford in these years.

First, the army, which could always be relied upon to provide an eager
audience. In 1787, one play at the Hereford Theatre was performed 'by
desire of the Officers of the King's Own, or 3rd Regiment of Dragoons';
in 1790 another was 'by desire of the Officers of the Herefordshire
Militia', and one in 1801 'by desire of the Officers and Gentlemen of the
Hereford Volunteers'. Other performances were given by desire of pupils
or former pupils of Hereford School: one, in 1790, by 'the young
gentlemen of the College School', and another in 1801 by 'gentlemen
educated at Hereford School'.

Then there were the clubs. The 'Gentlemen of the New Inn Clubs'
were the patrons of a performance in 1791 of a comedy, *Such Things Are!*;
the 'Gentlemen of the Catch-Club' (a catch club was a form of singing
club) were the patrons for *The Suspicious Husband*; the 'Gentlemen of the
Mitre Tavern' for Macklin's *Man of the World*, and the 'President and
Members of the Thursday card-club at the New Inn' for *She Stoops To
Conquer*—all three of these were benefit performances in March 1796.

Most intriguing of all was the Munchausen Society, whose members
patronised another performance, in October 1801, of *Such Things Are!* This
society was presumably formed by fans in Hereford of Baron
Münchausen's *Narrative of his Marvellous Travels and Campaigns in Russia*,
published in 1785. A contemporary bestseller, this book was full of extraordinary and most improbable stories about Baron Münchausen, a
German nobleman who had supposedly served in the Russian army against
the Turks; his stories, together with equally improbable ones from other
sources, were collected into a book. One of the stories, to give a flavour of
the book's zany absurdity, is of the Baron having the misfortune to be swallowed by a fish. Finding its stomach less than agreeable, he dances a hornpipe, causing the fish great pain; it opens its mouth to cough out whatever
is making its insides sore, whereupon the Baron escapes.

A few performances at the Hereford Theatre were patronised by
masonic lodges, such as one in 1790 performed 'by desire of the master

MR. GIBBON,

Who, with the utmost respect, begs leave to solicit the patronage of the Ladies and Gentlemen of HEREFORD, and its vicinity, on this occasion, which will ever be remembered with the strictest sense of gratitude.

THEATRE, HEREFORD.

On WEDNESDAY, DEC. 2, 1801,

Will be presented, the celebrated COMEDY of

NOTORIETY.

Ned Nominal, Mr. GIBBON.
Colonel Hubbub, Mr. SHUTER.
Sir Andrew Acid, Mr. CHAPMAN.
Lord Jargon, Mr. CHAMBERS.
Clairville, Mr. FARREN.
Saunter, Mr. G. SHUTER.
James, Mr. RANDALL.
And Blunder O'Whack, Mr. FOX.

Honoria, Mrs. EDWARDS
Lady Acid, Mrs. CHAMBERS.
And Sophia Strangeways, Mrs. GIBBON.

IN THE COURSE OF THE EVENING,

A Comic Song, by Mr. FOX.

A Favourite Song, by Mr. EDWARDS.

A New Song, by the Youngest Miss SHUTER.

After which, a Favourite INTERLUDE, called

HOB IN THE WELL;

OR, THE HUMOURS OF A COUNTRY WAKE.

Sir Thomas Testy, Mr. CHAMBERS.
Friendly, (with a Song,) Mr. EDWARDS.——Old Hob, Mr. RANDALL.
Young Hob, Mr. G. SHUTER.

Flora, Mrs. GIBBON.
Old Hob's Wife, Mrs. CHAMBERS.——Betty, Miss SHUTER.

To which will be added, that truly laughable FARCE,

All the World's a Stage;

OR, THE SPOUTING BUTLER.

Charles Stanley, Mr. GIBBON.
Harry Stukely, Mr. FARREN.
Sir Gilbert Pumpkin, Mr. CHAMBERS.
Cymon, Mr. G. SHUTER
Watt, Mr. RANDALL.——Will, Mr. E. SHUTER.
And Diggory, (the Spouting Butler,) Mr. SHUTER.

Miss Pumpkin, Mrs. CHAMBERS.——Miss Kitty Sprightly, Mrs. GIBBON.
And Betty, (the Tragedy Housemaid,) Miss SHUTER.

TICKETS to be had, and Places for the Boxes taken, of Mr. GIBBON, at Mr. Kyrwood's, Widemarsh-street.

WALKER, PRINTER, HEREFORD.

Playbill printed on silk for a benefit performance at the Hereford Theatre,
2 December 1801

and brethren of the Palladian Lodge of Free and Accepted Masons', in which Shuter, himself a freemason and now called 'Brother Shuter', spoke a prologue 'descriptive of the rise, progress and uses of Masonry'. Mr. Charlton (another of the leading actors in the company) was also a freemason, and the fact that two of Watson's actors were freemasons gives an indication of the respectability of their profession. The whole programme of this particular evening was devoted to freemasonry, the main play being *The Brothers*, by Richard Cumberland.

The season usually lasted from December until March, but the theatre sometimes opened at other times as well, to coincide with the Assize Week—either in March or August—and the Race Week in July or August, and sometimes for the May Fair. Each season would have a certain number of susbscription nights, and there would usually be a new play each night throughout the season.

The season would always end with a series of benefits, usually for the actors, but now and again for others connected with the theatre. In Hereford there were benefits for Mr. Day and his wife, the fruiterers, or

Theatre, Hereford.

For the Benefit of Mr. CHALMERS.

☞ Mr. CHALMERS' engagement having clofed on his Benefit night, a renewal of it, for the refidue of the feafon, was completed at the requeft of Mr. Watfon :---He therefore, with infinite refpect, begs leave to acquaint his friends and the public, this Second Benefit is his only Emolument for that latter agreement.-----And from the many folicitations Mr. C. has received to produce an ENTIRE PANTOMIME on this occafion, he thinks it his duty to accommodate his patrons to the extent of his power. But as they muft be fenfible no fuch reprefentation can be produced with the leaft convenience or propriety, while any of the audience are on the ftage, this cannot of courfe be complied with : and in order to make up the deficiency fuch a regulation muft produce in the receipts of the night, Mr. C. hopes it will not be thought an intrufion in thus catering for the accommodation of his friends, that nothing but Full Price, at any part of the night, can be received from any perfon ; nor can any one whatever, on any pretence, be admitted behind the fcenes during the evening's performance.

On FRIDAY, JAN. 11, will be prefented,
THE COMEDY OF
THE SUSPICIOUS HUSBAND.
The part of Ranger, by Mr. CHALMERS.
End of Act II. (by very particular defire)
The PARAPHRASE on Shakefpeare's SEVEN AGES,
By Mr. CHALMERS.
To which will be added,
An ENTIRE PANTOMIME, called
BLUE BEARD;
OR,
HARLEQUIN'S ANIMATION.
In which will be introduced
THE ANIMATION, GLADIATOR, DYING,
AND
SKELETON SCENES.
To open with, an exact Reprefentation of
A FALL OF SNOW.
Harlequin, Mr. CHALMERS.
With a variety of LEAPS and ESCAPES.
The whole to conclude with,
A LEAP THROUGH A BRILLIANT SUN
OF VARIEGATED FIRE,
By Mr. CHALMERS.
☞ TICKETS to be had at the ufual places; and of Mr. CHALMERS, at Mr. Gammon's, Byeftreet.

A benefit performance advertised for 1792

42

orange sellers, at the theatre, as well as for Mr. Parker, the builder of the theatre, and later, in 1819, for Mr. Meredith, the box keeper; this was an important job since on popular nights competition for boxes could be stiff. Often a star performer would take part in the benefit of a fellow actor, charging a low fee and raising the level of takings substantially. In some cases the money was sorely needed, as in one benefit in Hereford for Mr. Warner, an actor who had been imprisoned for debt. The play-bills normally announced that tickets could be bought either from the theatre or from the actor himself, giving the address where he was staying—more often than not rooms above a nearby shop.

Like other provincial theatre managers, Watson would hire well-known actors from London or elsewhere to act alongside the regular cast, playing the roles they had made famous in the metropolis. The rest of the cast in 1786 consisted of Watson's own company—Messrs. Shuter, Charlton, Weston, Harvey, Buckle, Bishop, and Withington.

Performances would usually begin between 6.00 and 6.30p.m., and would generally start with a musical item. The curtain would then rise and one of the company would speak the prologue; after this would come the main play of the evening. This in turn was followed by entertainment of some kind; anything from a musical interlude to singing, acrobatics, dancing, reciting, or even fire eating. The evening's entertainment would finish off with a farce or some other light piece, often with musical numbers. After eight o'clock it was usually possible to get in at half price; the evening would generally conclude by ten o'clock, but often continued much longer.

The repertoire in Watson's theatres included a number of Shakespeare's plays, such as *The Merchant of Venice, Hamlet, Othello, Macbeth,* and the comedies *As You Like It* and *Measure for Measure;* Sheridan's plays *The Rivals, The School for Scandal,* and *Pizarro;* Goldsmith's *She Stoops to Conquer;* and spectacular melodramas like *The Castle Spectre* and *Bluebeard;* there were some topical plays, such as *Democratic Rage, or Louis the Unfortunate.* Other popular plays included *The Beaux's Stratagem, The Clandestine Marriage,* and *Inkle and Yarico.* There was a large repertoire of farces and other short pieces, such as *The Wonder! or A Woman Keeps a Secret, Bon Ton,* or *High Life Above Stairs* (by Garrick) and *Scrub's Travels,* performed by George Shuter, who added topical references to the town in which he was playing. In between these plays there were always a selection of interludes, songs, dances and jigs, some of them perhaps survivals of an older repertoire based on folk tales, as for example the 'dwarf dance with a whimsical transformation into Mad Moll', that was included in one performance in Leominster in 1836.

The theatre in Hereford attracted good audiences, but while the standard of acting was praised, the lighting and the standard of cleanliness were not. Watson was notoriously parsimonious, and was said to burn 'kitchen stuff in place of oil, which is very offensive'. A letter in the *Hereford Journal* on 28 January 1789 complained that

> It was the worst lighted theatre – to say it was a theatre! – and the dirtiest eyes ever beheld. A general gloom pervaded the whole house, the lights were half out before the entertainment was well begun, and from the first it was evident that the stage had been a scene of common resort from the street for the few preceeding hours, not having that day been honoured with a brush. What renders this inattention less excusable, there hung proper lamps round the house, the stage &c., but all dark, all dismal. A scarcity of oil could surely not be the reason; and for the boards being left in that filthy condition on the entrance of the audience, it can hardly be imagined that the manager of the King's Company would not afford his theatres closing with the appearance of common cleanliness.

The manager of the King's Company was in fact unwell at this juncture, and perhaps unable to attend to these matters in person—the same edition of the *Hereford Journal* included an apology that extreme illness prevented him waiting on his patrons. The season in Hereford had now ended, and the company moved on to Leominster.

When Watson's company—now sometimes known as the Hereford and Cheltenham Company of Comedians—were not playing at the Hereford Theatre, it was sometimes used by other entertainers. These included a troop from the Royal Circus in February 1792; Dr. Katterfeltro, who came to Hereford in August 1794 to exhibit his solar microscope, powerful magnets, and other attractions; and a series of three lectures in 1802 on the science and practice of elocution, first for the stage, second for the pulpit, and third on 'the importance of elocution as a social accomplishment, and its connection with the relative duties of polished life'. Another somewhat puzzling show, in 1806, was an exhibition of 'Philosophical Fireworks'.

In 1796 John Richer came to the Hereford Theatre. Richer was a famous young dancer and acrobat whose performances of dancing on a tightrope at Sadler's Wells Theatre had recently drawn the fashionable crowds. In Hereford he was to repeat the performance he had given in royal courts all over Europe, consisting of manoeuvring on the tightrope with a hat and two flags; on a later occasion he was to 'play on the violin

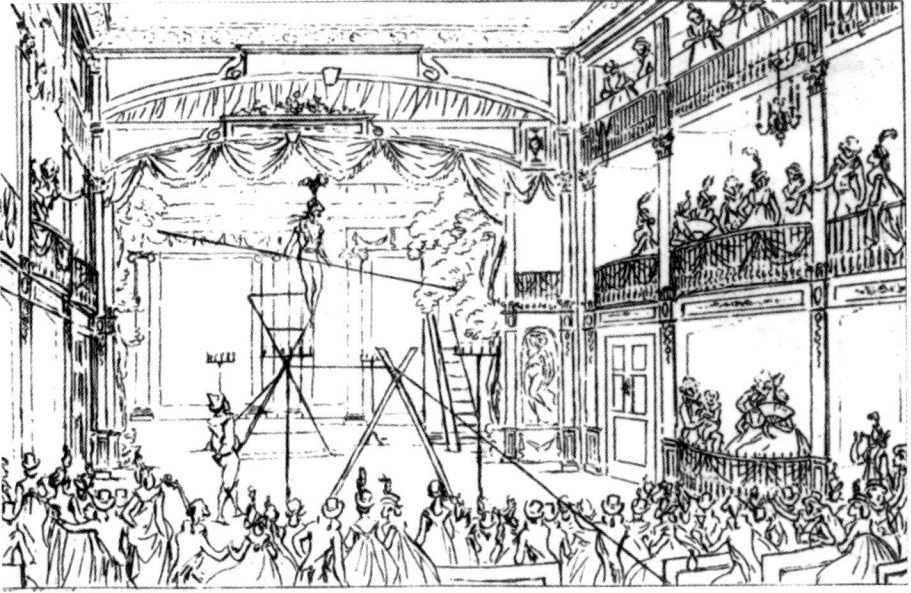

An etching from 1795 showing John Richer performing his famous leap from the rope at Sadler's Wells

in various attitudes while dancing on the rope, and take a leap backwards over a man's head'.

The following week Richer directed a performance of *William Tell*, 'the most admired and popular entertainment ever performed at Sadler's Wells'. Four years later he gave up his tightrope walking and married Watson's daughter Louisa; Watson soon afterwards made him manager of his Stroud theatre.

The 1796 season, now ending, had been a great success. In fact Watson announced in the *Hereford Journal* that it had proved the best season he had ever experienced anywhere. The last week of the 'stock business'—that is, not including the benefits—included a performance of *The Merry Wives of Windsor*, and to advertise it Watson—well practiced at penning verses for suitable occasions—inserted a short poem in the *Hereford Journal*:

Falstaff's Card

To the Friends of Sir John this card he sends greeting
Inviting them all to next Thursday night's meeting.
Tho' no Dancers on Ropes or famed Bruisers to fight
He presumes that his fare will please tastes less polite.
If good sense and fine writing their palates can hit,

He has plenty of those and good room in his pit.
In Broad Street he'll open a house to receive 'em,
And place on his table what will not deceive 'em.
Should the public be pleased in his larder to look,
Many dainties they'll find and Will. Shakespeare's the cook.
> Pray Ladies peruse
> This part of the News
> To rational fare I invite ye
> Where great Shakespeare's art
> Will touch the soft heart
> And Falstaff in Love will delight ye.

In England in the 1790s, the war with revolutionary France prompted exuberant displays of patriotism. One evening in January 1798, a play called *The Jew and the Citizen* was performed in Hereford in celebration of the queen's birthday, 'by desire of Mrs. Whitmore ... with songs appropriate to the occasion, and effusions of loyalty'. A little vignette of this lady has been preserved for us, because long afterwards, in the 1860s, an aged theatregoer looked back at the 'palmy days of the theatre in Hereford', when Watson was still manager. The theatre was, she recalled, 'well patronised by the most distinguished families in the city and county. ... A kind but very eccentric lady (Mrs. Whitmore) made it a point to have no private engagement on the nights of performance, and rarely omitted to fill her accustomed place in the boxes. At the moment of her entry the curtain was raised, and the National Anthem was given by the whole dramatic corps, in which she heartily and artistically joined'. Another performance in Hereford later in the season, on 12 October, took place shortly after news had arrived of Nelson's victory over Napoleon's fleet in the Battle of the Nile. The evening included a series of patriotic songs, one written by a gentleman to the tune of *Hearts of Oak*, and Watson announced that the entire receipts of the performance would be 'added to the voluntary contributions for the support of the widows and orphans of those brave fellows who fell in the glorious victory obtained by Admiral Nelson over the French fleet'.

In August 1798 Watson, who was in poor health, entered into a partnership with Richard Hoy, a member of his cast resident in Worcester, who now took over responsibility for the running of the Hereford and Worcester theatres, until he and Watson parted in 1803. For the new season the theatre was given boxes, an improvement which had long been desired. These boxes would have run around three sides of the auditorium, below the gallery; the side boxes were usually seen as the special preserve of the ladies, but patrons would usually have taken their places in the middle boxes. Those buying tickets for the boxes had to make sure their names were written down in the box plan, held by the keeper of the box office, an important individual.

The beginning of the 1798 season on 1 August coincided with the Assize Week in August, and for this week Hoy secured the presence of Sarah Siddons, in Hereford as part of a tour which included Cheltenham, Gloucester and Worcester. Now aged 43, and at the height of her fame, Sarah Siddons, would have remembered Hereford from her younger days, though back in 1771, at the age of 16, she would have performed in the temporary theatre at the Swan and Falcon. She had left her father's company back in 1774 and spent a few years in the provinces after a disastrous debut at Drury Lane in 1775. As a more experienced and confident actress she had returned to London in 1782 to act in Garrick's play *Isabella*, and this time her performance had been an overwhelming success. Mr. Symonds of Pengethley, near Ross, who happened to be in London at the time was one of the many who saw Sarah Siddons' performance. In a letter to a friend back in Herefordshire he wrote with enthusiasm that he had just seen the first actress in the world, who had made the ladies faint, although he went on to joke that actually it was the fashion to stop the performance by fainting, and that it was rumoured that someone was planning to set up a fainting school.

There is no doubt that Sarah Siddons had a quite extraordinary

Theatre, Hereford.

R. Hoy presents his most humble respects to the Ladies and Gentlemen of Hereford and its vicinity—informing them, with all due deference, that, having entered into Partnership with Mr. WATSON, and being now Acting Manager of the Theatre, he will make it his unremitting study to deserve their favour and protection by every possible exertion; and he is happy to announce that

Mrs. SIDDONS,

Is engaged for the Assize Week.

This, with the addition of Boxes (which has been long desired) will, he humbly hopes, please and accommodate every class of the supporters of the Theatre.

On WEDNESDAY EVENING, AUG. 1, 1798, Will be presented, the Tragedy of

JANE SHORE.

The Part of JANE SHORE, by Mrs. SIDDONS. To which will be added,

THE SPOIL'D CHILD.

During Mrs. Siddons.'s Performance—Boxes, 5s. Pit, 3s.—Gallery, 2s.
Nothing under Full Price can be taken.
Tickets and Places for the Boxes to be taken of Mr. G. SHUTER, at the Theatre, from Ten till Two o'clock.
Doors to be opened at Half-past Five, and to begin at Seven o'clock.

Mr Hoy respectfully informs the public that his greatest ambition is to shew every respect to the city of Hereford, by a strict attention to the business of the stage; and as the admittance of any one behind the Curtain must be injurious to the performance of the evening, he makes known, that no one can be admitted behind the Scenes on any pretence whatever.
And in order to prevent any mistake on the Nights of Performance, it is earnestly requested that Tickets may be taken at the time Ladies and Gentlemen enter their Names in the Box-Book, which must be done on the day preceding each Performance; or such places as are taken previous to that day will be considered as given up, and the Box-Keeper at liberty to let them to others — No more Tickets will be issued than the Boxes can conveniently hold — Those who have Places are requested to send their Servants to keep them by Half-past Five o'clock.

effect on audiences; faintings among the sensitive were commonplace, in that age of refined sensibilities. Completely absorbed in the character she was playing, she had the effect of an emotional tornado. Her voice was remarkable, strong and sweet, with 'the melancholy yet shattering tones of a nightingale'; 'her voice is naturally plaintive, and a tender melancholy in her level speaking denotes a being devoted to tragedy. Yet this seemingly settled quality of voice becomes at will sonorous or piercing, overwhelms with rage, or in its wild shriek, absolutely harrows up the soul'.

Sarah Siddons as the Tragic Muse, by George Romney, 1783

Silhouette of Sarah Siddons as Euphrasia, by Lady Elizabeth Templetown

When she returned to Hereford, ticket prices for her performances were far higher than the usual—5s. instead of 3s. for the boxes, 3s. instead of 2s. for the pit, and 2s. instead of 1s. for the gallery— and there were strict instructions that those who had booked boxes should send their servants at opening time, 5.30p.m., to make sure that places were reserved.

The five plays Sarah Siddons performed in Hereford included most of the roles for which she was famous, though not that of Lady Macbeth, regarded as her most celebrated. She played Jane Shore in Rowe's play of the same name, about a strong and outspoken woman seduced first by Edward IV, whose mistress she became, and then by Lord Hastings. She became a pawn in the power struggles of Richard, Duke of Gloucester (later Richard III) for the throne; ultimately betrayed and reduced to abject poverty, she died a tragic death. Siddons also played Calista in Rowe's *The Fair Penitent*, another story of a strong-minded woman ultimately defeated by cruel fate; like *Jane Shore*, this was the sort of sentimental tragedy, full of high-flown language, that appealed to 18th century theatregoers. She also played Isabella in Garrick's version of Southerne's *The Fatal Marriage*—the part which had brought her to fame back in 1782; Mrs. Beverly in *The Gamester* by Susannah Centlivre; and Lady Randolph in *Douglas* by the Rev. John Home, a celebrated tragedy based on an old Scots' ballad.

Sarah Siddons was regarded as the best tragic actress of the day, but where comedy was concerned Elizabeth Edwin was considered pre-eminent. Mrs. Edwin was acting at the Theatre Royal in Bath at this period, and in the following month, September 1798, Hoy booked her to appear in Hereford for six nights, where she played in *As You Like It*. Hoy was evidently keen to bring to Hereford the most famous players of the day, and three years later he managed to secure the appearance of Sarah Siddons's brother John Philip Kemble, for the week beginning on Monday, 27 July 1801. Kemble was to play *Hamlet*, and for this week ticket prices were raised, as for Sarah Siddons's performances, with the boxes now 5s. instead of 3s. Kemble, 'the first actor in the world', was acknowledged as the finest tragic actor of the day, grand, noble and intense, as captured in a painting of him in the role of Hamlet in contemporary court dress, with a gown of rich black velvet (see illustration alongside).

Sometimes criticised for his stiffness, somewhat orotund delivery, and his apparently rather idiosyncratic pronunciation, comedy was not John Philip Kemble's forte; as Charles Surface in *The School for Scandal* he was said to be 'as merry as a funeral and as lively as an elephant'. But he and his sister became the founts of what was known as 'the Kemble religion'. William Hazlitt said of Kemble: 'We think the distinguishing excellence of his acting may be summed up in one word – *intensity*; in the seizing upon some one feeling or idea, in insisting upon it, in never letting go, and in working it up, with a certain graceful consistency and conscious grandeur of conception to a very high degree of pathos or sublimity'.

John Philip Kemble in the role of Hamlet

Now, at the turn of the century, the Hereford theatre was at the height of its popularity, well patronised by the nobility and gentry and able to attract the very best actors in the country. In 1806, 20 years after the opening of the theatre, Watson retired completely, and Hoy for a time became sole manager.

CHAPTER VII
Theatres in Leominster, Kington, Ross & Ledbury

In the early 18th century Leominster had a small theatre in Burgess Street, its site later occupied by a fire station. Later, the town was on John Ward's circuit, and Ward performed there in 1757 for a 12-week season, in a theatre fitted up in the Schoolhouse in Church Street (originally the Forbury Chapel). In 1789 Watson renovated the theatre, announcing that it was 'now neatly fitted up and rendered much more regular and commodious than heretofore'. The 1789 season lasted eight weeks, from February to March, with performances on Monday, Wednesday and Friday. There were subscription nights, as in Hereford, with a new play each evening.

On 19 February 1794, on their next visit, Their Majesties' Servants performed the tragedy of *Democratic Rage, or Louis the Unfortunate*, (see illustration overleaf) complete with an exact model of the guillotine and a procession of the king to his place of execution. In this performance the part of Marat was played by Mr. Gill, later one of John Crisp's actors. At this stage the Leominster Theatre was managed by William Miell, a former circus superintendent whom Watson had appointed as manager of part of his circuit. Miell also managed the theatres at Wolverhampton, Shrewsbury and Worcester until he died in 1797, employing his own actors. Leominster, though, was visited by Watson's own company in 1796 'at the express request of the principal families' there, after it had played in Kington, so Leominster evidently received visits from both companies. After Miell's death Leominster reverted to Watson's circuit. Leominster also had its fair share of visiting performers who leased the theatre when it was not in use by the regular company; one such was Lee Sugg, a celebrated ventriloquist, who came to Leominster in 1801 after performing in Hereford; from Leominster he went on to Bromyard. John Crisp, who took over the Leominster Theatre with the rest of Watson's circuit, brought some of his visiting 'London stars' on to Leominster from Hereford, among them Master Betty, the 16-year-old Shakespearean actor whose appearance on the London stage had caused such a sensation three years before. Betty played in Leominster for three nights in September 1807.

The patrons of the Leominster Theatre, like those in Hereford, included a variety of regiments, clubs and individuals. In June 1801 the gentlemen of the Leominster Volunteer Cavalry patronised a performance featuring John Richer performing his famous rope walk. Later, in 1836, a play was performed under the patronage of the gentlemen of the Monday Nights Club.

The Leominster Theatre may have been popular, but the *Leominster Guide* of 1808 had grave doubts about its morality: 'There is no regular theatre in Leominster. The building appropriated to that use is the Courthouse, situated in Church Street, where dramatic representations are generally performed every third year, when the manager of the Hereford theatre has permission from the bailiff and capital burgesses to perform about 40 nights. The receipts, when the house is full, amount to about £40. So great has been the rage for visiting this popular source of amusement that the wives of the labouring poor of this town have pauned [*sic*] a part of their

Theatre, Leominster.

BY THEIR MAJESTIES' SERVANTS.

On WEDNESDAY Evening, Feb. 19, 1794, Will be presented, a TRAGEDY, in Four Acts, (never performed here) called

DEMOCRATIC RAGE;

OR,

LOUIS THE UNFORTUNATE.

As performed upwards of thirty nights, with unbounded applause, at the Theatre-Royal, Dublin.

Louis (King of France,) Mr. WESTON.
Kerfaint, Mr. FOWLER.
D. of Orleans (otherwise Egalité,) Mr. ROBERTS.
Sieyes, Mr. EDWARDS.
Petion, Mr. BLANDFORD.
Robespierre, Mr. SMITH.—Marat, Mr. GILL.
Cleri, Mr. EYRE.—Paris, Mr. TOMS.
Dauphin, Mrs. EYRE.
Queen of France, Mrs. EDWARDS.
Princess Royal, Miss SMITH.
Princess Elizabeth, Mrs. SMITH.

In Act the IVth.

THE PROCESSION OF THE ROYAL MARTYR TO THE PLACE OF EXECUTION,

With an exact MODEL of

THE GUILLOTINE.

AND

AN ELEGY ON HIS DEATH,

Written, and to be spoken, by Mr. EYRE, in the Character of Cleri.

To conclude with, " God save Great George our King."

TO WHICH WILL BE ADDED,

A COMEDY, in Three Acts, (never performed here,) called

LOVERS' QUARRELS.

(As altered from the MISTAKE, and now performing at the Theatre-Royal Covent-Garden, with great applause.)

Sancho, Mr. MIELL.
Jacintha, Mrs. VALE.

No admittance behind the Scenes.
To begin exactly at Half-past Six o'clock.
Days of playing, Monday, Wednesday, and Friday.
Vivant Rex et Regina.

☞ Mr. MIELL *particularly requests that all demands upon the Theatre, may be sent in weekly, that the same may be regularly discharged.*

Newspaper advertisement for 1794

52

wearing apparel, and even the intended dinner of their husbands, for the purpose of personal accommodation. The manager receives and merits good encouragement by engaging performers of respectable abilities'. By 1801 the theatre had boxes, and tickets, as in Hereford, cost 3s. for boxes, 2s. for the pit, and 1s. for the gallery. The theatre seems to have become less popular in the ensuing years, and the labouring poor perhaps even allowed to eat their dinner again, because by 1819 ticket prices had dropped to 2s. for boxes, 1s. for the pit and 6d. for the gallery.

By 1819 the company at the Leominster Theatre, known as the Hereford Company of Comedians, was under the management of the ever-popular George Shuter. Actors sometimes supplemented their salaries by giving lessons in elocution and anything else they happened to be good at, and this probably explains why a performance on 21 April 1820 included 'a hornpipe by a young lady of Leominster' together with 'the celebrated wooden shoe dance by Mr. E. Shuter'; the young lady had probably been taught by the popular George Shuter, a good hornpipe dancer, and his son followed her with a comic version, clumping away in his wooden shoes.

In June 1827 Charles Crisp announced that he had 'taken the Leominster Theatre, which will open newly painted and decorated, on the first Race Day'. The company would subsequently return to Leominster for a season of ten weeks, commencing at the end of

The Forbury Chapel in Church Street, Leominster,
once the site of the town's theatre

October. This was now the normal pattern for most provincial theatres, which would open for the Race Week, and the Assize Week if there was one, and return for the main season of up to 60 days at some point between October and April. The patron for the Race Week was always the steward of the races.

Often the London stars who visited Hereford would come on to Leominster. William Charles Macready performed in Leominster for one night in May 1829, and the following year the popular comedian Charles Mathews came also for one night, in August, to perform his one-man show *Mr. Mathews will be at Home.* Writing to his wife (who was staying with a friend in Ross while her husband was performing in the county), Mathews sounded less than impressed by the Leominster Theatre, though complimentary about the audience: 'Such an affair – no boxes to the house! Poor Crisp "thought there would be a great gallery" – ha, ha, to me! Highest price 2s, we had £15, fourteen of which was pit (or boxes) – really genteel people'. It seems, therefore, that there must have been at least 140 people in the pit, and only 20 people in the gallery, paying 1s. each. It also seems that the boxes—which had been installed at the turn of the century—could be removed or replaced depending upon the popularity on the show.

In 1836 James Rogers, the new manager of the Hereford Theatre, came to Leominster for a season with an entirely new cast, and it was they who performed a fashionable new farce, *Catching an Heiress*, on 23 November 1836. The characters were:

Tom Twigg (a Whitechapel'r, 'a wild young thing' who was
    not born yesterday, possessing an extensive knowledge
    of the polite arts and fashionable sciences)   Mr. Bellair
Baron Sowercroutzensausengen (a Yarman minstrel –
    possessing the O–E–I–O–E in beautiful perfection)   Mr. Bellair
Captain Poodle (a Cavalry Officer possessing all the usual
    military accomplishments)   Mr. Danneville
Captain Killingly (his friend and comrade, possessing
    the same qualifications)   Mr. Bouverie
Mr. Gayton (a respectable elderly gentleman possessing
    a respectable fortune and a handsome daughter)   Mr. Turner
Stubby (a facetious waiter, possessing a talent for invention) Mr. Tyler
Caroline Gayton (a supposed heiress, daughter of the
    respectable elderly gentleman; a young lady
    possessing great powers of attraction)   Miss Cooke
Mr. Fip Gayton (An Exquisite Exclusive, possessing every
    attribute of puppyism)   Miss Cooke

Sally Giggle (Miss Gayton's maid, a young person
     possessing many useful as well as ornamental qualities) Mrs Rogers
Jessamy (Miss Gayton's Tiger – a lad possessing a good
     stock of impudence and various Tiger accomplishments) Mrs Rogers

Performances at the Leominster Theatre, however, were becoming rarer and rarer. In 1842 Mr. Henderson, manager of the Ludlow Theatre, engaged a 'London Star', Miss Waylett, to appear at Leominster, raising ticket prices to no less than 4s. for the boxes. Two years later came an unusual spectacle, *Zildorhaskan, or the Lion of Tartary*, in which the part of the lion was played by a dog called Bruin, clothed in a lion's skin; the docile Bruin was celebrated for his faithful portraiture of the lion's character. After 1859 performers started to use the newly built Leominster Corn Exchange, and from this time the Forbury Chapel reverted to other uses.

In Kington the earliest theatre was in a barn at the back of the Sun Inn, now demolished (its location is uncertain). Performances were confined by the magistrates to 36 nights, and takings were usually only about £20, no more than about half those of the Leominster Theatre.

John Ward came to Kington in 1758 for an 11-week season, and it was during this stay that Sarah Kemble gave birth to her son, Stephen, shortly after leaving the stage when playing Anne Bullen in *Henry VIII*. Tradition has it also that during this season Sarah Siddons gave her first performance at the tender age of three. After taking over from Ward, Roger Kemble came to Kington periodically, and two members of his company, Mr. and Mrs. Masterman (later to set up their own strolling company), were married in the town in 1775.

John Boles Watson made periodic visits to Kington. His first one was probably in November 1785, where a member of the audience wrote that His Majesty's Players were 'the best travelling company I ever saw'. Two months later they were back, on their way to Leominster. The company's next visit was not until 1791, and then again in 1796. A report in the *Gloucester Journal*, from this date, illustrates just how popular theatregoing was among the gentry, and the extent to which the players depended on their patronage. It was from a man who 'wishes to make mention, in the most favourable light, of a set of Players, which he found in the small town of Kington, Herefordshire, where to his great surprise the houses were crowded night after night with some of the first Nobility and Gentry, and the company countenanced to an astonishing degree of liberality. The same correspondent states that the Comedians are just now removed to Leominster, at the express request of the principal families there and thereabouts, and there is no doubt, from the established regularity of Mr. Watson's Company, his short stay, go where he will, and a superlative elegance of his scenes, dresses &c., but that the same success will attend him and his performers in their present quarters'.

By this time Watson was performing in a theatre fitted

Advertisement from the Hereford Journal, *1802, for a performance in the barn theatre at the Talbot Inn, Kington*

up in the King's Head, which stood on the site of the market house. One 1796 performance, for which a playbill survives, was for the benefit of a Kington clockmaker, Mr. Skarratt, who went on stage to dance a hornpipe, preceded by his son who, most impressively, danced a hornpipe, blindfolded, over 16 eggs; a daughter was also roped in to give an address of thanks. Soon after this a new theatre was fitted up in a barn (also now demolished) behind the Talbot Inn in Bridge Street. It had a pit and gallery, but no boxes.

The patrons of the Kington theatre were, as in Hereford and Leominster, professional groups or clubs, army officers, masonic lodges, as well as individuals. In 1791, the tragedy of *Charles I* was performed 'by desire of the Silurian Lodge of Free and Accepted Masons', two of the actors, Shuter and Charlton, being masons themselves. 'Brother Charlton' sang a masonic song, while 'Brother Shuter' spoke a prologue 'descriptive of the rise, progress, and uses of masonry'. Other patrons were 'the young gentlemen of the Grammar School', and J.G. Cotterell Esq. Later the theatre benefitted greatly from the patronage of a wealthy local woman, Lady Coffin Greenly, of Titley Court, whose diary records one occasion in 1818 when a benefit was held for one of the actresses, Mrs. Davies, under her patronage; the performance included the musical play *Guy Mannering*, adapted from a novel by Sir Walter Scott, and Garrick's farce *Miss in her Teens* (see illustration opposite). Lady Coffin Greenly wrote in her diary that 'the house was the fullest that had been. £25 15s. 0d. was taken, and more than £5 of persons were turned away for want of room'. This was an impressive sum, particularly since the performance took place during a violent heatwave. The audience could well have numbered as many as two or three hundred. This performance included the notorious Charles Waldegrave, who also ran his own theatre company, well known for its lax morals. Quite why he was acting with Crisp's company is not clear. In the same year a certain Mr. O'Brien, a penniless manager of a Welsh strolling company, arrived in Kington from Llandrindod to put up play-bills but, unable to pay for them himself, had to solicit a few shillings from a friend.

Few of the London stars who appeared in Hereford, and sometimes in Leominster too, made their way to Kington. Some did, though; John Richer came in 1802 to perform his tight-rope walking, and later on the actor Tony-le-Brun. In August 1832 Chin Lao Lauro, from Drury Lane and Vauxhall Gardens, appeared in Kington; the playbill announced that he would 'dance a hornpipe on his head, and conclude with a wonderful extension on the backs of two chairs in imitation of a spread eagle, and at the same time throw brass balls in various directions'. Later that year there was a falling out of some sort among the management; Mr. Harmond, the manager, seems to have been sacked without notice, but enlisted the help of the local gentlemen of Kington and Leominster to stage a performance.

In 1836, the Kington Theatre was taken over and redecorated by Mr. Saunders, an actor in the Hereford company, for a season which included performances of *Richard III* and *The Merchant of Venice* starring the nine-year-old child prodigy, Master Calhaen, as Shylock. The theatre was renovated again a few years later, in 1842, by a new manager, Mr. Clifford, but like so many other theatres it was used less and less by this time. It closed, and was eventually demolished.

While both Leominster and Kington enjoyed regular visits to their flourishing if small theatres, Ross was not so fortunate. No doubt there were many unrecorded visits, but only a handful are known about. In the 1740s a band of players led by the Irish actor Richard Elrington visited Ross; John Ward came for three weeks in 1761, and in 1791 John Boles Watson came for a short season in May and June, performing in a theatre fitted up in the town hall, now the market house. It would have made a small, dark theatre, with the view of the stage obscured

> LAST NIGHT BUT ONE.
> For the Benefit of Mr. and Mrs. *SHUTER.*
>
> ————
>
> THEATRE, TOWN-HALL, *ROSS,*
> *On Thursday, June 2, 1791, will be presented,*
> *A BOLD STROKE FOR A WIFE,*
> *WHO'S THE DUPE,*
> AND
> *PATRICK IN PRUSSIA,*
> OR, LOVE IN A CAMP.
>
> ————
>
> *Last night of performing this season,*
> On Friday, June 3, 1791, will be performed:
> *KING RICHARD THE THIRD,*
> AND
> *BARNABY BRITTLE,*
> OR, A WIFE AT HER WIT'S END.

An advert for a benefit performance for Mr. and Mrs. Shuter at Ross in 1791

by a row of columns down the middle of the room. In fact only the front few rows of the pit and the side boxes nearest the stage can have had an uninterrupted view. Watson's performances there included *The Gamester* by Mrs. Centlivre, on 11 May, and *Richard III*, on 3 June.

In June 1829 a theatre was fitted up in Ross by Thomas Mildenhall, an actor and scene painter in John Crisp's company. Presumably he renovated the former theatre in the market house. Mildenhall had collected together a group of relatively distinguished actors—from the Edinburgh, Manchester, Plymouth and Liverpool theatres, and from the Olympic Theatre in London—in order to do a summer tour of Ross, Ledbury, Monmouth, Chepstow and South Wales. He announced in the *Hereford Journal*:

> Mr. Mildenhall, Manager, has the honour of announcing to the Nobility, Ladies and Gentlemen, and the Public in general of Ross

and its Vicinity, that he has at very considerable expense fitted up a Theatre in a most superior manner. The inside Roof is entirely hid by Arches thrown over and tastefully decorated, so that nothing remains offensive to the eye. The Boxes are elegantly fitted up with crimson furniture, and the seats newly stuffed and covered. The Wardrobe is of the most splendid description, together with the Scenery and Decorations, which are all new, and the company of established celebrity.

Mr. M. during the short season he will have the honour of remaining in Ross, will produce on a very superior scale the greatest novelty, and humbly trusts that his exertions, which are and will be stretched to the utmost to secure the approbation of a discerning Public, may meet with a portion of that indulgence it will be his greatest pride to acknowledge.

The season will commence on Tuesday evening, June 16th, 1829, with Sheridan's admirable play of Pizarro; or The Spaniards in Peru.

Mildenhall was giving a somewhat rosy picture of his theatre. Robert Dyer, Mildenhall's stage manager and one of his 'established celebrities', was markedly less enthusiastic:

'Vain pomps and glories of the world, I hate ye', I exclaimed when I entered the Ross theatre; I felt that an extraordinary portion of fortitude was necessary to the endurance of its miserable dimensions, rendered, no doubt, more apparent, by the remembrance of Drury-lane and Covent-garden; but, by persuading myself that I did hate the pomps and glories of the theatrical world, I became at last reconciled to their opposites. Besides, Ross is a beautiful neighbourhood, and the seasons of blossoms and flowers was ripening into fruits and seeds, and I felt content in my station, by thinking my peregrination a summer pleasure excursion.

Mildenhall was relatively well off but lost a lot of money in this theatrical venture. He evidently paid his actors well, since for Dyer this season was the most profitable of all his theatrical engagements, though it brought him 'to the theatres-rural, with all their primitive comforts'. As well as being a scene painter, Mildenhall was a good singer and a good actor in low comedy; and furthermore he had 'the happy facility for writing songs and dramas of a local or temporary nature'. He had, according to Dyer, an unfortunate condition, which was that he was very short-sighted—a major handicap, one would think, for a scene painter. 'Some of his friends having complained that he passed them without notice, to prevent such charges of neglect ever after, he nodded indiscriminately to all he passed, to the great amusement of those acquainted with the infirmity of his nature'.

Tickets in Ross cost 3s. for boxes, 2s. for the pit, and 1s. for the gallery. Mildenhall began the season with Sheridan's popular tragedy *Pizarro*, in which the Peruvian leader, Rolla, is defeated in battle by Pizarro. Next, the company performed *The Man of Ross*, Mildenhall's dramatisation of the life of John Kyrle, for nine nights, and then followed up this success with another of his compositions, *The Red Barn, or Midday Murder*. On 26 June they performed *The Rivals* by desire of Colonel Crawford of Goodrich, and on 24 July *The Belle's Stratagem* by desire of 'several ladies and gentlemen'. This performance included, as usual, a variety of songs, dances and other little trifles: the favourite song 'I'll be a Butterfly' by Mrs. Lockwood, followed by The Frog Dance by Mr. Dipper, and 'an address written expressly for the occasion by a Lady of Ross'; finally Miss Walton danced a sailor's hornpipe.

The last night, 19 August, began with a farce, *Love Laughs at Locksmiths, or The Yorkshireman's Disaster*, followed by another farce, this one written by Mildenhall, entitled *We Are All Ruined, or Love, Flowers and Butterflies*. Altogether they played in Ross for two months, but according to Dyer they were 'not attractive' in the town, although a report commented that 'propriety of behaviour in the actors' domestic habits has removed the odium which the irregularities of others had unfortunately entailed on the profession in the town'. Now and again the Hereford company performed in Ross—they came for a season in 1836—but who these more disreputable strollers were is not known.

John Ward's company visited Ledbury in 1752, where their performances of *Henry VIII* were well patronised by the gentry, and again in the following year, by which time Ward had bought 'a large quantity of modern and Roman habits so that the characters may be properly dressed'. Neither Kemble nor Watson seems to have visited Ledbury, but in 1829, Mildenhall and his company came to Ledbury in August, after their mixed success in Ross, and fitted up a theatre in New Street—this could have been in the former George Inn, opposite the Talbot. All the scenery, props and adornments would have been taken from one town to the next, and the Ledbury theatre was fitted up in the same way as that at Ross: the inside of the roof was 'entirely covered in a novel and handsome manner, an arched ceiling having been thrown completely over and tastefully decorated'; the boxes were fitted up with crimson furniture, and the seats stuffed and newly covered. The tickets, as in Ross, cost 3s. for boxes, 2s. for the pit and 1s. for the gallery.

The players began their season in Ledbury on 25 August, and stayed for two months. They were successful enough to attract a number of patrons, performing *The Belle's Stratagem* by desire of James Martin Esq. of Colwall, *The Honeymoon* by desire of E. Foley Esq. and *The School for Scandal* by desire of the Race Committee. For a performance of *Guy Mannering* they persuaded an amateur, or 'a gentleman, his first appearance on any stage', to take part. They performed the spectacular play *Timour the Tartar*, with Dyer as stage manager, and, four days later, Mildenhall's own composition, *The Man of Ross*.

Their performance in Ledbury was a great success. 'Ledbury made ample amends', wrote Dyer, 'for the failure of Ross; the houses, after the first night, were well filled by those whose critical taste made their applause an honour'. Dyer singled out a handful of people as particular friends: John Higgins and his wife, who worked to promote Dyer's interests; Thomas Ballard; and most particularly the Grundy family and their daughter Mary Ann, whose friendship was 'the chief source of my private pleasures'. It was a friendship which was to lead to great sadness a few years later. After this success, Mildenhall, Dyer and their fellow actors parted from Ledbury 'as from our home'.

Mildenhall returned to Ledbury in January 1831 for a season of six weeks, bringing with him a different cast, including some from Hereford. This time they performed in the town hall (the market house) with 'good fires constantly kept' to provide some heat. The patrons this time included Colonel Drummond of Underdown, and 'the Bachelors of Ledbury'. Mildenhall started with the melodrama *Black-Eyed Susan*, and another amateur from the town was found to go on stage, appearing as Shylock on 14 January. The following week, on 17 January, Mildenhall announced that 'impressed most gratefully by former favours', he would donate the receipts of the night to 'the fund for purchasing the Butcher Row' (a reference to the Society for Effecting the Removal of the Butcher's Row), and in aid of this good cause the gentlemen of the Ledbury Musical Society had volunteered their assistance. For the performance Mildenhall had been presented with a new painted backcloth representing the street outside the Butcher's Row.

The Friday evening, 21 January, saw the second appearance of the amateur, whose performance as Shylock had been received enthusiastically; this time he played Othello. Mildenhall's great surprise, though, was reserved for the end of the month: on 31 January he proudly announced the appearance of 'the most singular novelty in the theatrical world, an Actor of Colour'. This theatrical novelty was Ira Aldridge, the African Roscius (Roscius being the name of an eminent Roman actor), who was touring the provinces prior to appearing at Covent Garden the following season. Ira Aldridge was a so-called 'free black', born in New York in 1807, reputedly of Senegalese royal blood. After acting as an amateur in the African Theatre in New York, he had come to England in 1823.

Aldridge stayed in Ledbury for three nights, appearing in *Slave, or the Blessings of Liberty*, and, on his last night, as Rolla, the heroic Peruvian leader defeated by Spanish conquistadors, in Sheridan's *Pizarro*. At the end of this performance he delivered a farewell address written expressly for the occasion, driving home the plight of slaves and his hopes of freedom for them; and printed copies of the address were given to members of the audience as they entered the theatre. Aldridge's visit came at a time of intense public agitation, led by the evangelical Christian lobby, in favour of the abolition of slavery—just a few months previously the *Hereford Journal* had printed a letter calling on the Mayor of Hereford to organise a petition to parliament on the subject—and the Anti-Slavery Society referred to Aldridge's majestic presence on stage as a signal contribution to the struggle for abolition (slavery was finally abolished in all British colonies in 1834).

In Ledbury, Aldridge, who had a fine singing voice, also sang a song entitled 'Opposum Up a Gum Tree'. This song had become a favourite in England after the comedian Charles Mathews had included it in his show *A Trip to America*. Mathews related the story as follows:

> The black population [in America] being in the national theatres under certain restrictions have, to be at their ease, a theatre of their own. Here he [Charles Mathews] sees a black tragedian perform the character of Hamlet, and hears him deliver the soliloquy 'To be or not to be, that is the question, whether him nobler in de mind to suffer or lift up him arms against a sea of hubble bubble, and by opposum end 'em'. At the word opposum the audience burst forth; 'Opposum! opposum! opposum!' On enquiring into the cause of this, Mr. Mathews was informed that 'Opposum Up a Gum Tree' was the national air, or sort of 'God Save the King', of the Negroes, and being reminded of it by Hamlet's pronunciation of 'opposing end them', there was no doubt but that they would have it sung. The opposum ... is addicted to climbing up the gum tree, thinking no-one can follow him; but the racoon hides himself in the hollow of the tree, and as the poor opposum goes up, pulls him down by the tail; and that is the plot. The cries of 'Opposum' increasing, the sable tragedian comes forward and, addressing the audience, informs them that he will sing their favourite melody with his greatest pleasure, and actually sings it.

THEATRE, MARKET HOUSE,
LEDBURY.
BY PERMISSION OF THE MAGISTRATES.

For TWO NIGHTS ONLY.
FOR THE BENEFIT OF

MR. DYER,
(LATE STAGE MANAGER).

All men are subject to vicissitudes, and it is a pleasing and a proud feeling, when in the hour of trial, a man can conscientiously say, my vices or my underservings are not the cause of this. Such is the case with Mr. DYER—after leaving Ledbury, a course of complete success was terminated by his engagement at Norwich, one of the first provincial circuits, and he there confirmed the favourable opinion entertained of his ability by his kind friends here. In that circuit he might have continued, but he received a more advantageous offer from the manager of the Newcastle Theatre, which he accepted, and a prospect of fame and fortune appeared before him, when the afflicting CHOLERA MORBUS commenced its ravages at Newcastle, and, by preventing the opening of the Theatre at the appointed time, not only destroyed all his hopes there, but (from his notice to quit) drove him for the present from the Norwich circuit. Thus circumstanced, Mr. DYER throws himself on the kindness of his former patrons and friends, and he therefore begs to offer an Entertainment to the Ladies and Gentlemen of Ledbury and the vicinity; and he most respectfully solicits their patronage, assuring them their support will confer a great obligation, and ever be remembered with more than gratitude.

On Wednesday Evening, May 9th, 1832,

The Evening's Entertainments, will commence with an occasional Recitation by Mr DYER, (as spoken by the celebrated Mrs. SIDDONS), in which he will give his

FIVE REASONS

For appealing to the liberality of his Friends and the Public.

Reason the *first*, stand forth—*(enter the eldest son)*—a goodly boy,
The father's pride, a mother's anxious joy;
Come in my *second* reason—*(enter the eldest girl,)*—do I hear
The enlivening plaudit, the benignant cheer ?
Enter a *third*—*(enter second son)*—more tender still in years—
And now my *fourth* (*enter second girl*)—not least in love appears.
A *fifth* I can produce—but spare its age—
A three month's actor on this " wide world's stage : "
Oh! let her rest in all an infant's charms,
Where she lies pillowed in her mother's arms !
These are the *reasons*, these the motives keen,
That urge my efforts in the toilsome scene ;
And, if I know our frame, they stand confest
In every mother's—every father's breast.

After which, a Dramatic Entertainment (in two parts), called

SCENES OF THE PASSIONS,

Selected to display the varied passions of Jealousy, Parental Love, Revenge, Conjugal Authority, and an Actor's Life; and in which the several characters will be arrayed in the correct costume, appropriate to the scenes. In the course of the entertainment, Mrs. DYER will sing many favourite and popular songs.   The scenes selected are from the admired Comedy of

The Wonder! a Woman keeps a Secret.

Don Felix,....Mr DYER   Donna Violante,......Mrs DYER

The celebrated Play of

VIRGINIUS, THE ROMAN FATHER.

Virginius,....Mr DYER   Virginia,....Mrs DYER.

SONG. --- "PLAIN GOLD RING," BY MRS. DYER.

The fashionable Comedy of

THE HONEY MOON.

Duke Aranza,..Mr DYER   Lopez,..Master DYER   Juliana,..Mrs DYER
SONG.==="RISE GENTLE MOON," BY MRS. DYER.

Maturin's celebrated Tragedy of

BERTRAM; or, the CASTLE of St. ALDOBRAND.

Bertram,....Mr DYER   Imogine,....Mrs DYER
BRAVURA.---" THE SOLDIER TIR'D," BY Mrs. DYER.

And the laughable Sketch of
SILVESTER DAGGERWOOD, the STROLLING ACTOR.

Silvester Daggerwood,...Mr DYER,   Authoress,..Mrs DYER

Incidental to the Second Part, an admired Ode on
THE DEATH OF NELSON.

PART II.---AN EXTRAVAGANZA CALLED—

Soon after this the season finished, and Mildenhall returned to his former job as actor and scene painter for John Crisp. Meanwhile Robert Dyer, Mildenhall's stage manager in 1829, returned to Ledbury in 1832 in unfortunate circumstances. Dyer had been offered a job at the prestigious Newcastle Theatre, having acted on the Norwich circuit for a time, and his career seemed to be prospering. However, the Newcastle Theatre was forced to close because of a cholera outbreak in the town, and Dyer was left without work or any means of subsistence.

In order to support his wife and growing family, now five strong, Dyer wrote an entertainment to be performed by his wife and himself, consisting of excerpts from a variety of different plays. The family embarked on a tour of provincial theatres, and were glad to find their performances well received. In May 1832 they arrived back in Ledbury; Robert Dyer was especially pleased to

*Above and previous page: The Dyers' performance
of excerpts from a variety of plays, as advertised
for performance in Ledbury*

renew acquaintance with the Grundys, and 'the affectionate attention of Mary Ann assumed a more ardent character'.

The Dyers' performances in Ledbury took place in an atmosphere of political ferment. 'The news of the return of Earl Grey to office arrived in Ledbury on the afternoon of my last performance, and the whole town being politically deranged, I was desired to postpone my entertainment to the following night. My friend's [Mary Ann's] earnest advice determined me, and she passed a joyous evening with my family'. The following night, a terrific storm blew up, and Dyer wondered whether to postpone his last performance again, but in the end decided to go ahead. He was in the dressing room of his lodging house when he was stunned to receive a message that Mary Ann had died. She had left home and joined a large party of friends all going to the theatre, but had collapsed in the street. This tragedy cast a pall over the remainder of Dyer's stay; 'the death of my friend entirely destroyed my prospects in Ledbury. I could not play in a sepulchre, and her untimely fate cast the gloom of the grave over the dejected town, and even the extreme kindness of my friends could not alleviate my distress of heart and mind'. At the request of Mary Ann's brother, Dyer composed an epitaph for her memorial tablet before he left the town.

Ledbury was also visited periodically by a section of the Hereford company who now performed at Kington, under their manager Mr. Saunders; in 1834 they came for a short season, performing among other items *Catherine Audley, or the Recluse of Ledbury*, a play based on a local legend. Saunders returned to Ledbury in 1836, this time with the nine-year-old child prodigy Master Calhaen, who played Richard III and Macbeth. In 1847, James Rogers, manager of the Hereford Theatre, visited Ledbury for a season. But as in other towns, the theatre in Ledbury was becoming less popular, and performances grew steadily fewer.

CHAPTER VIII
The Crisp Brothers and their Successors

In 1806 Robert Hoy took over as manager of John Boles Watson's circuit. He did not remain as sole manager for long and the following year took into partnership a young actor called John Crisp. Still in his early twenties, Crisp was an enterprising man, keen to expand the circuit, and two years later he bought Hoy out.

In the summer of 1808, the young Edmund Kean joined the company for a few months, acting first in Cheltenham, then in Warwick. In Warwick Kean was given some major roles, but when the company moved on from there to Birmingham, a more important theatre, Crisp hired better-known actors for the major roles, and Kean was consequently demoted again. Not happy with this, he accepted an offer from the manager of a touring company in Carmarthen whither, not having any money, he and his wife trudged.

As under Watson's management, the Hereford Theatre was hired out on occasion. In May 1809 it was used by Mr. Lloyd to give a course of three astronomical lectures featuring his dioastrodoxon, or grand transparent orrery. This enormous orrery, or model of the solar system, was 21 feet in diameter, and for the occasion was surrounded by an assemblage of appropriate scenery. 'The whole for magnitude of scale, grandeur of design, and varied beauty [said the advertisement], infinitely exceeds any thing of a similar description in this, or perhaps in any other country'. It was also the only popular astronomical instrument admitted into the University of Oxford. Tickets for the three lectures were 10s. 6d., including printed notes.

Crisp was an energetic manager, and soon set about hiring increasing numbers of 'London stars' to appear in Hereford for two or three nights. He expanded the circuit he had acquired in 1807—at times it took in Birmingham and Chester—and now and again the company would split temporarily into two, one half going off to visit the farther-flung theatres of the circuit. In 1813 John Crisp's brother George appeared at the Hereford Theatre, and in 1815 the youngest brother, Charles, joined the company. Charles became Acting Manager in Hereford when John was away either touring other parts of the circuit or acting in London, and in 1821 he effectively took over as manager in Hereford.

In 1807, and again in 1812, John Crisp brought Master Betty, the former child star, to Hereford, and the following year Stephen Kemble, the fourth of the Kemble siblings to go on the stage. Stephen did not share the talents of the other Kembles, but went on to become the respected manager of the Newcastle Theatre. In 1810 John Bannister, a gifted mimic and a highly popular comic actor, came to Hereford, to give his famous one-man show *Bannister's Budget, or an Actor's Ways & Means for 1810*. Called the Budget because it was devised to bring in money, it was a series of short pieces, such as a study of extreme old age which he called 'The Superannuated Sexton', and 'Two ways of telling the same Story – by a Clergyman and a Boatswain'. Bannister's father, a comic actor in Garrick's company, had been born in Newland in the Forest of Dean.

On 27 February 1816 John Crisp organised a grand celebration to commemorate the one hundredth anniversary of Garrick's birth. In the morning, and at intervals throughout the day, the bells of the city were rung. At four o'clock in the afternoon a public dinner was served in the great room of the Hotel (the City Arms), with the mayor presiding, and with a military band playing appropriate airs. Tickets were 12s. 6d. for a full meal with port and sherry. After the meal came the toasts, 16 in number:

1. The King, Queen, Prince Regent, and all the Royal Family.
2. The memory of David Garrick (*a bumper* [a generous glassful])
3. Prosperity to Hereford, the birthplace of Garrick.
4. The memory of the late Chief Steward of Hereford, a distinguished Patron of the Drama, and a Friend to this commemoration [the Duke of Norfolk, who had hoped to attend].
5. The health of the present Chief Steward, whose absence is occasioned by his parliamentary duties.
6. The memory of Kate Clive.
7. The memory of Mrs. Siddons, the best *tragic* actress of her day.
8. The memory of Mr. Powell, a native of this city.
9. The health of Mrs. Edwin, the best *comic* actress of her day.
10. The memory of Samuel Foote, who was descended from the Goodyeres, of Burghope, near this city – *song*.
11. The health of Mr. John Kemble, the best *tragic* actor of his day.
12. The memory of Roger Kemble, the Father of the Flock, and a Native of this City.

13. Mr. Charles Kemble, and the rest of the Family.
14. The memory of Nell Gwynne, a native of Hereford – *song*.
15. Old England and her Drama, in Town and Country.
16. Success to Mr. Crisp, and thanks to him for suggesting the present meeting.

Kate Clive (1711-1785), or Kitty Clive, was one of the leading actresses at Drury Lane. A coquettish Irishwoman, her exuberant humour and 'nimble pertness' made her a natural comic actress. She was jealous of Garrick's ability, and is reputed to have said, 'Damn him! He could act a gridiron!' Conversely, Kitty Clive was said to be the one person of whom Garrick was afraid. Her connection with Herefordshire is unclear; presumably her husband George Clive, a barrister—from whom she separated soon after their marriage—was from the county. Rumour had it that Kitty Clive had once acted in Hereford, though this seems improbable.

If Kitty Clive's connection with Herefordshire is obscure, Samuel Foote (1720-1777) had a much closer, though rather grisly, association with the county. Foote became famous as an actor and as the author of popular farces which mocked and satirised targets as various as politicians, artistic pretensions, methodism, and incompetent doctors. He became manager of the Haymarket Theatre in London, and though his brilliantly funny but libellous plays attracted endless lawsuits, Foote kept his theatre open, and managed eventually to obtain a 'summer licence' for it—at the time only Drury Lane and Covent Garden had full licences. Foote was also a very funny actor, whose extravagantly *outré* performances of Othello and Hamlet were never forgotten by those who saw them. Dr. Johnson once said of him that 'I resolved not to like him but the dog was so very comical that I was obliged to lay down my knife and fork, throw myself back upon my chair, and fairly laugh it out'.

Samuel Foote's mother, Eleanor Goodere, was the sister of Sir John Goodere, a bachelor who lived at Burghope House, at the foot of Dinmore Hill. Sir John was on bad terms with his younger brother, Captain Samuel Goodere, and threatened to disinherit him in favour of his sister, Eleanor. An enraged Samuel Goodere caused his brother to be kidnapped at Bristol, and then to be strangled by two sailors on board the man-of-war which he commanded. The deed was immediately discovered and Samuel—who had succeeded as 3rd baronet on his brother's death—was tried, convicted, and hanged in Bristol in May 1741. After the murder, Burghope House gained the reputation of being haunted, and later in the century was sold for building materials. Of Samuel Goodere's two sons, the eldest died insane. The greater part of the Goodere estate passed to his sister, but Samuel Foote also inherited a substantial fortune, which he dissipated in a short space of time in the cause of setting himself up as a man of taste.

Following the 16 toasts in celebration of these varied connections, Crisp gave a short speech in honour of Garrick, and then

> soon after seven, the whole of the company adjourned to the Theatre, which was illuminated, &c. with great spirit and liberality by the Manager, Mr. Crisp. On the outside a splendid star in variegated lamps decorated the front, and over the door was a transparency, representing a portrait of Garrick, with suitable devices – Within, the front of the Boxes, and that of the Stage, were ornamented with festoons of flowers tastefully disposed, intermixed with variegated lamps, the dome was also decorated in like manner, and the whole of the Theatre, crowded with a circle of smiling beauty, presented a *tout ensemble* highly gratifying to the eye … Notwithstanding the enlargement of the boxes, which had the best effect, every place was taken.

In addition to enlarging the boxes, Crisp had created a separate entrance to the pit.

The performance at the theatre began with Susannah Centlivre's *The Wonder! or a Woman Keeps a Secret*, the last play in which Garrick had performed; this time William Charles Macready played the part of Don Felix. Next came Sheridan's *Monody on the Death of Garrick*, spoken by Charles Crisp, followed by *The Jubilee*, written by Garrick for his Shakespeare commemoration at Stratford in 1769, and performed at Drury Lane when the original was rained off. This performance in Hereford included a version of Garrick's Drury Lane procession, 'representing the leading characters from Shakespeare's various plays, with appropriate banners and devices, surrounding a full-length transparent portrait of Garrick, supported by the tragic and comic muse'. The procession and all the performances 'went off with the greatest eclat'.

Generally Crisp opened the theatre for the Assizes and the Race Week, in July and August; in some years he came briefly in the spring too. In 1818 the theatre underwent some further improvements; the interior was painted, new lamps and chandeliers installed, and the seats provided with stuffed cushions; the pit passage was also widened. For the 1819 season John Crisp divided his circuit in two, as Watson had done previously, and created two separate companies; the Hereford Theatre was to have a 'dramatic corps new to the city', with the exception of a handful of actors from the old company. John Crisp's brother Charles was appointed Acting Manager to look after the theatre in his absence.

On 25 January 1819 an anonymous 'young lady'—an amateur—of Hereford played the part of Juliet, to great acclamation. The young lady, later revealed as the 17-year-old Miss Howe, was given her own benefit on 19 February, and after playing Jane Shore came on stage to speak an epilogue, written by 'a gentleman of Hereford'. She was dressed as Nell Gwyn on the occasion when she had first captivated Charles II, while speaking an epilogue to a play by Dryden and wearing a hat the size of a large coach wheel (see p.14). Miss Howe's epilogue went as follows:

Lord, where am I! – what strange sight now appears –
Why sure I've been asleep a hundred years!
Things look so odd, so alter'd, and so queer,
I really have forgot why I came here.
Oh, let me think, 'twas just once more to see
The long-left place of my nativity:
Alive or dead, in heaven or in earth,
Still shall I love the spot that gave me birth,
Still shall the unerring monitor within
Bound to you all, and claim you for its kin!

Well, bless me, what a Proteus thing is dress,
Quite chang'd; such pretty – odds – I can't express.
I never dreamt to meet with aught so dashing,
And really hop'd you'd think *me* in the fashion.
Lord, what a pretty hat; do give it me,
I'll give you mine instead, if you'll agree;
Tis true 'tis somewhat *small*, but (let me say),
You see 'twas made against a *rainy day*.
You laugh – but in this very hat ('tis true),
I've pleased a *King*, and surely may please you.

(Takes off the hat)

O may you, in this vandalising age
Still prove the polish'd patrons of *the stage*,
Rescue the drama from its threaten'd death,
Where Siddons learn'd, and Garrick first drew breath!
Foster young genius, modest worth requite,
And fan the smother'd ember into light!
Chase from the timid bosom every fear,
And give the world one Garrick every year!

And now, before I leave, I think I might
Just say a word on what has pass'd tonight:
And first – Miss – What-d'ye-call-her-name – Miss Howe,

A sprightly lass, I saw her but just now,
She begg'd of me that in her name I'd say,
How poor were words your kindness to repay;
How weak, how vain, were aught that she could do,
To cancel the great debt she owes to you;
Yet she returns you *thanks* (as her poor part),
Warm from the breast, and faithful from the heart!
Glowing, yet guileless, fervent, yet sincere;
And hopes to do the same *another year*.

Perhaps, my townsmen, you would wish to know,
What I think of this youngster, this Miss Howe;
Really, she's a smart girl, but it's a pity
That one so young, so thoughtless, nay so *witty*,
Should misapply her talents and her time,
In striving to attain where few can climb.
She play Jane Shore, the tame, affected elf –
I could have play'd it quite as well myself,
Although I've been this hundred years, and more,
Strange to the stage, to poetry, and Shore.
And when her *Roxalana* you shall see,
I think your judgement will with mine agree,
She'll play it *beautifully*, I dare say,
Ha! Ha! – but yet I should not laugh this way –
I ought to recollect she's but *seventeen*,
And she may *mend* perhaps, *such things have been*.

And now, my friends, farewell – may ever joy
Wait you, and happiness without alloy;
I go *aloft, there* is *my* place of bliss,
And those may follow me, who're tir'd of *this*.

By this date performances would quite often include songs with a local theme, as in a performance of 19 March 1819 which included 'John Lump's Peep into Hereford', a comic song with descriptions of different parts of the city; and a comic tale called 'The Christmas Pie, or the Whimsical Freak of the Sutton Farmer at Bullingham Wakes'. A performance the following week included George Shuter, the son of Watson's actor, singing 'Old Hereford's a Wonderful Town O!'.

In 1822 John Crisp gave up the management of his circuit. It had become so big as to be unwieldy, and he had over-extended himself financially; in 1819 he had bought the Cheltenham Theatre, equipping both it and the Worcester Theatre with gas lighting; then in 1821, in a stroke of bad luck, the Shrewsbury Theatre, which must have been very shoddily built, collapsed. Part of the circuit was sold, and Charles Crisp became manager of what was left, including the Hereford Theatre. Later, in 1830, John formed another small company of his own, which performed at Leominster and some of the other smaller theatres in the circuit.

In 1824 Charles Crisp undertook more improvements to the Hereford Theatre, including a new proscenium and new drop scenes, one a copy of the Covent Garden drop scene, and the other a view of a street scene in Hereford. The renewed popularity of the theatre is reflected by a short-lived journal, the *Hereford Weekly Reporter, or Theatrical Looker-On*, written anonymously and published weekly throughout the 1824 season, from January to June. The season started well; one of the first performances of the year, under the patronage of the High Sheriff, 'produced a bumper; the boxes displayed a truly brilliant assemblage of beauty and fashion'.

Most of the author's comments were approving, but there were some plays which left him unimpressed. One such was *Timour the Tartar*, a play full of spectacle involving horses on stage scaling ramparts, leaping waterfalls, and making flying leaps through breaches in castle walls. The paper grumbled that 'real horses and real water are so much before our eyes daily that they do not attract much of our notice at night'. He was highly impressed, though, with a dragon breathing real fire in *The Wood Demon*; 'there is something wonderful in the composition of this newly invented greek fire'. Some of his criticisms were not altogether serious; commenting on a production of *Henry IV* he complained that Bardolph's nose was too small: 'Falstaff's allusions to Bardolph's nose would have been more impressive had that promontory been larger in appearance, and decorated with a few carbuncles or meteor-like exhalations'.

His station was in the pit, evidently a dangerous place at times; in one performance he was 'near being wounded by a piece of the glass chandelier which fell a sacrifice to the

---

THE HEREFORD

WEEKLY REPORTER,

OR

THEATRICAL LOOKER-ON:

FROM APRIL 5TH. TO JUNE 7TH. 1824.

HEREFORD :

PRINTED AND SOLD BY JOHN PYNDAR WRIGHT,

BROAD STREET,

1824.

PRICE 1s.

sabre of Mr. Henderson, who seemed to commence an attack in a truly soldier-like manner'. This was bad enough, but he also had to contend with peas thrown by unruly elements in the gallery. He commented: 'We were glad to see the seats of the gods so well filled and their excellencies in such good humour. Bye the bye, as we sometimes take our seats in the pit, we beg to address our prayers to the divinities above alluded to, that they will not be so profuse in their blessings in the form of pease, which are all very well in the shape of a pudding – or (in their element of soup) in the *pit* of the stomach; but are really very hard of digestion in their crude state in the *pit* of a theatre'.

Another 1824 performance was acted by desire of 'a lady of our town of great distinction', and to accommodate her wishes the manager had replaced the scheduled play with the lady's favoured piece. How much notice the cast were given we are not told, but the number of plays they had to commit to memory is astonishing; each performance still included a serious play and a farce or melodrama, interspersed with songs, hornpipes or other entertainments; and the programme changed every day. In the course of the 1824 season, from 25 March until 7 June, no fewer than 63 plays were performed.

At the end of the season the anonymous writer of the *Hereford Weekly Reporter* was more than satisfied; it had been, he said, 'the most successful season for the last 15 years, and proves that the exertions of a most respectable body of performers regulated by private conduct and professional talent under the jurisdiction of a spirited manager must succeed; and we sincerely hope to witness on a future season the same company, for a better we do not think can be found in any provincial establishment'. However, he was disappointed that Charles Crisp had not hired a single London star during the season, in contrast to his less cautious brother: 'it may be remarked by many that during the whole season the manager has not in one instance gratified the town by the temporary engagement of any celebrated London Actor (or *stars* as they are called) and we own the circumstance has often excited our surprise; but we have now ascertained that it is a principle of the present management to avoid these engagements as injurious to the interests of his own company'.

The theatre had been well patronised for most of the season, although on one evening the anonymous author arrived at the theatre at the usual time to see a performance of *Richard III*, and found the building locked up and in total darkness. It transpired that the audience 'at the usual time of beginning was composed of so few that the manager deemed it unnecessary to give the actors trouble, it being a night introduced out of the regular order of succession, so dismissed the house'. This was an exception, however, and the *Hereford Weekly Reporter* was encouraged that the popularity of the theatre, and the increasing circulation of his journal, meant that 'the prejudice against the Drama once existing in our city is rapidly declining'.

By now most patrons were individuals, such as the High Sheriff, the member of parliament for Hereford, or gentry from the surrounding area such as Sir John Cotterell, Sir Hungerford and Lady Hoskyns, Edward Bolton Clive, and Lady Emily Foley. Some of the patrons, however, were still groups, such as the stewards of the steeplechase, 'the legal professional gentlemen', 'the medical professional gentlemen', and the members of the Herefordshire Foxhounds. One performance in 1824 was by desire of Captain Biddulph and the Officers of the Herefordshire Yeomanry Cavalry, and another in 1831 by desire of Colonel Sir George Cornewall and the officers of the Herefordshire Regiment—this performance enlivened by the playing of the regimental band. Back in 1807 another performance had been given by desire of the non-commissioned officers and privates of the 1st Regiment of the Hereford Volunteer Infantry, an indication of the theatre's wide social appeal.

Amateur performers would sometimes appear on stage with the professional company, and these 'gentlemen amateurs' would be given star billing on the playbills, such as one advertising a performance of *Henry IV* in Hereford in 1826. Here, although Henry IV himself was played by John Horton, Charles Crisp's leading actor, three of the most prominent roles were assigned to 'gentlemen amateurs, who move in the highest circles of fashion', their recognised position in society apparently outweighing any consideration of their acting abilities. In fact, according to Robert Dyer, gentleman amateurs were, 'with few exceptions, the worst of the amateur genus'. In his opinion 'men from the middle grade of society make the best artists, because a feeling of degradation does not wither their energies, and their knowledge of life gives a portraiture, not a burlesque, on nature'.

John Horton was also known for writing a play entitled *Nell Gwynne; or the Red Lands of Herefordshire*. Other actors in Charles Crisp's company included Mr. Vining, the stage manager, Miss Quantrell, later to marry Vining, Mr. Waldron, a good tragedian, Mr. Thompson, 'an excellent representative of old men', and Mr. Gill, 'really unctuous in low comedy'. A Hereford theatregoer remembered Gill's playing of Autolycus in *The Winter's Tale*, and of the Clown in *Twelfth Night*, as being 'as racy as it could be'. Crisp's two daughters, Eliza and Cecilia, were also members of the company. Crisp himself was a noted Paul Pry, a popular 'nosey-parker' character, constantly poking his nose in when he wasn't wanted; his words 'I hope I don't intrude' became a popular catchphrase.

In September 1829 Madame Vestris performed at the Hereford Theatre, now newly lit with gas. A young singer very popular in 'breeches parts' owing to her legendary legs, Madame Vestris became famous in the 1830s and 40s as manager of the Olympic Theatre in London, where she staged spectacular extravaganzas. Madame Vestris performed at Hereford together with her sister, Miss Bartolozzi, as well as Miss Ellen Tree, the future wife of Charles Kean. The following summer saw the appearance in Hereford of the highly popular comedian Charles Mathews who performed his one-man entertainment *Mathews's Comic Annual for 1830*. A brilliant comic actor, in appearance Mathews was very tall and thin. He had an extraordinary ability to change his appearance, voice and manner utterly from one moment to the next, so much so that his audiences often had difficulty in believing they were watching a single person. His shows would consist of fast-moving sketches in which he would play perhaps eight or ten characters. The audience in Hereford were treated to the story of Mr. Sadjolly's trip to London to see Mr. Polish the dentist, assorted characters such as Sir Benjamin Blancmange, a kirk story 'Fifthly, my brethren', and songs such as 'The Country Concert'. Mathews's shows, or 'monopolyogue' entertainments, had many imitators, among them W.S. Woodin and Mr. and Mrs. Howard Paul, but none of them could match Mathews's virtuosity.

In 1830, William Charles Macready appeared at the Hereford Theatre again for three nights—back in 1816 he had taken part in John Crisp's Garrick centenary celebrations in Hereford. An eminent tragedian like John Philip Kemble, Macready had the same serious approach to the roles he played. Dyer wrote that 'as an actor he is faultless, for he conceives with judgement and executes with truth. He is Virginius, and Hamlet, and Tell, as completely as if the souls of his heroes had entered him when he assumed the garb of each character'. Macready is also often regarded as the first director in the modern sense. In 1837 he became manager of Covent Garden—to be succeeded in turn by Madame Vestris —and was well known for his careful rehearsals and his supervision of every aspect of his productions.

The week before Macready's appearance at the Hereford Theatre, Charles Kean appeared there for three nights. Charles, the son of Edmund Kean, was a respected actor but without his father's manic personality. Among Charles Kean's roles in Hereford was that of Sir Giles Overreach in Massinger's *A New Way to Pay Old Debts*; (see illustration overleaf), his father's performance of this same role is said to have reduced Byron to convulsions, and to have disturbed his fellow actors with its manic communication of evil. Charles Kean became better known as manager of the Princess's Theatre in London in the 1850s, where he produced lavish productions of Shakespeare.

In 1831, Charles Crisp retired as manager of the Hereford Theatre; he

Theatre, Hereford.

THE Manager has the honour to announce an Engagement with the celebrated

MR. KEAN, JUN. !!!

For Positively Turee Nights only.

On Thursday Evening, May 6, 1830, Shakespeare's Tragedy of KING RICHARD III. Richard, Duke of Glocester, Mr. KEAN, Jun.—Friday, May 7, Sheridan's PIZARRO. Rolla, Mr. KEAN, Jun.—Saturday, May 8, Mr. KEAN's BENEFIT, and *Last Night*, A NEW WAY TO PAY OLD DEBTS. Sir Giles Over-reach, by Mr. KEAN, Jun. After which, THE HUNTER OF THE ALPS. Felix, by Mr. KEAN, Jun.

On Monday, May 10, the Manager has the pleasure of announcing an Engagement for most positively *Three Nights only*, with the justly celebrated and popular Actor,

MR. MACREADY,

on which Evening, Monday, May 10, VIRGINIUS. Virginius, Mr. MACREADY.—Tuesday 11th, HAMLET. Hamlet, Mr. MACREADY.—Wednesday 12th, for the BENEFIT of Mr. MACREADY, and his Last Night, OTHELLO. Othello, by Mr. MACREADY.

died the following year. The theatre had flourished under his guidance, attracting some of the best-known stars of the day, but after his retirement a succession of managers came and went, and intervals between perfomances became longer and longer. It is difficult to say exactly why this decline in popularity took place, but it reflected a wider change in attitudes, as an increasingly sober and high-minded age looked askance at the levity and immorality of the stage. Evangelical clergy had always distrusted the theatre, and according to one observer (in *Notes and Queries*, 1868) 'the fate of the drama within the city of the Wye may be attributed to the influence of the evangelical clergy when the late Rev. Henry Gipps, about thirty years ago, became incumbent of the united parishes of St. Peter and St. Owen'. Earlier in the century there had been virulent attacks on the immorality of the theatre; a pamphlet had been published in Hereford in 1819 entitled *Hints on the Evil Effects of the Stage*, and this was the 'threatened death' which Miss Howe had referred to in the verses quoted earlier. Readers of *Mansfield Park* (published in 1814) will know the extent to which respectable people could be appalled by the immorality and impropriety of many contemporary plays. Social habits were also changing; people were increasingly unwilling to sit through a whole evening's entertainment, lasting from six to ten o'clock, or even to midnight, in part because dinner was now eaten later. When the upper and middle classes did go out for an evening's entertainment, they chose increasingly to go to concerts and operas.

Crisp was succeeded briefly as manager by John Boles Watson junior, and then for a time by Mr. Macgibbon. In 1836 the theatre, now newly painted, was leased for the summer by Messrs. Rogers and Turnbull, who already managed a string of theatres in Birmingham, Newcastle, Cheltenham and elsewhere. In July they staged a new historical drama,

Burgehope House, or a Tale of Dinmore Hill, based on the gruesome story mentioned above. Another performance, in 1841, featured 'the Highly Trained Horse Xenophon':

Great Concentration
OF
ANIMAL TALENT!
THE HIGHLY
TRAINED HORSE
XENOPHON!

This splendid Animal has exhibited before HER MOST GRACIOUS MAJESTY and all the ROYAL FAMILY, on the 10th of October, 1841; also before a great number of the Nobility, who have expressed the greatest admiration. The late Mons. Ducrow, the first Equestrian in the World, has pronounced the Performance of this Horse as one of the rarest specimens of Training and Animal Sagacity ever seen.

1st   The horse will stand in the position of a Living Statue, Representing the Figure of the Horse bearing the Statue of King Charles.

2nd   Will stand with his Fore Leg over his Head, a position greatly admired by every Equestrian in the Kingdom.

3rd   Will tell the Time of Day by a Watch or Clock.

4th   Will draw a Cork from a Bottle and afterwards take the Bottle in his Mouth.

5th   Will stand upon two Chairs, bearing off Fore Leg and near Hind Leg on each Chair.

6th   Will select Pen, Ink, and Paper for the purpose of Writing a Letter, offering his Knee as a Desk, on which the Letter is written.

7th   Will take the Letter in his Mouth, knock at the Door, Ring the Bell, Deliver the Letter, and Return with an Answer.

8th   He will tell the value of any Piece of Money from a Sovereign to a Farthing, and point them out though covered with a Card.

9th   He will catch a Whip, Stick or Cricket Ball.

10th   He will pick from the table any Piece of Money that may be called for when indiscriminately placed before him, and carry it to his master.

11th   He will tell the number of Days, Weeks, and Months in a Year.

12th   He will Draw a Card from the Table that any Lady or Gentleman may call for.

13th   He will play at Put, Cribbage, or all-Fours with any of the Audience, and explain the same with as much correctness as Hoyle, who wrote them.

14th   He will Spell the Name of any one present.

15th   PICK UP AN EGG WITH A BIT IN HIS MOUTH, AFTERWARDS CATCH THE SAME.

16th   Will take a Handkerchief from the Person of any one near him.

17th   Will take a Handkerchief from various parts of his body.

18th   Will take the same from under his body, bending his head between his fore legs.

19th   Will catch the same in his Mouth, and return it to the owner.

20th   Will take a Hat off the Head of any one within his reach.

21st   Will calculate any Number in the Multiplication Table, from 1 to 144.

22nd   Will tell the Number of Points in the Compass, the different Quarters of the Globe, the Rising, Southing, and Setting of the Sun.

History does not record whether Xenophon, or the 'trained vixen fox' which appeared with him, lived up to expectations.

The theatre was used less and less by this time, but in 1843 it was leased for a season by a new manager, Charles Curling. From this date the building was intermittently known as the Theatre Royal, though quite how it gained this distinction is not clear. In January 1845 the theatre opened for three nights for an appearance by Ira Aldridge. Aldridge's appearance in 1831 in Ledbury has been told in the last chapter; after spending some years touring in the provinces he made his name on the London stage, becoming one of the outstanding actors of his day, and amassing a considerable fortune over the years. As well as appearing at Covent Garden and other London theatres he later spent much of his time touring the provinces with his own *corps dramatique*, driving them from town to town in an elegant carriage; one observer wrote that 'the coachman on the box, the flunkeys behind, and the distinguished-looking coloured gentleman inside attracted crowds as it leisurely roll'd along'.

The *Hereford Journal* commented, on 8 January 1845: 'Mr. Aldridge, the African Roscius, of whom the public have heard such frequent mention, made his bow to a Hereford audience on Monday night, and in this case we can truly and sincerely declare that the report has not exceeded the reality'. Aldridge gave a composite entertainment consisting of excerpts from some of his most popular roles, including Othello, Bertram, The Sicilian Pirate, and The Virginian Mummy (about a black waiter, Ginger Blue). He also sang the song of 'Jim Crow' three times to vociferous applause, introducing into it sundry comments about the occupations of the people of Hereford, 'the two public journals coming in for a share of the good-humoured sketch. Mr. Aldridge must have employed his time well in noticing all our little peculiarities'. ' Jim Crow', an early minstrel song, had been popularised by an American singer, Thomas Rice, who would perform a dance dressed as an old black man in ragged clothes, incorporating local issues and gossip into his song, and at the end of each verse dance the Jim Crow dance, singing:

So I wheel about,
I turn about,
I do just so,
And ebry time I wheel about
l jump Jim Crow.

Usually included in Aldridge's entertainment too was a piece he called 'England and the Negro emancipation; the slaves' gratitude', paying tribute to the anti-slavery movement which had led to its abolition in British colonies in 1834.

From 1853 onwards Aldridge spent much of his time touring in Germany, Poland and Russia. In Germany, where he was immensely popular, he spoke his lines in English, with a supporting cast speaking German. Showered with praise in Russia, where he was called the 'strolling missionary of art', he was created a baron in 1858 by the Duke of Saxe-Meiningen. Having been married twice, first to an English woman and secondly to a Swedish countess, he died in Lodz in 1867 while on tour in Poland.

Later in the same year, 1845, the Hereford Theatre reopened with a new cast under the management of Charles Poole and Hannay Charles. New backdrops had been painted by Mr. Gill, an enlarged band engaged under the direction of Mr. Ribbon, the interior had been renovated, and the seats recovered. Hannay Charles, as well as acting as co-manager, also turned his hand to writing plays, and on 10 November 1845 he staged *Hom Lacy and the Last of the Black Friars*, a new play based on a then prevalent local legend. Its characters included:

Viscount Scudamore

The Abbot of Dore, wizard of St. Cuthberts, smuggler of Foxley, and the last of the Black Friars of Black Friars Cross

Sydney Herbert, a young falconer of Hampton Court

Roger Phillpotts, grandson of the celebrated Roger Phillpotts of that name, of Narrow Cabbage Lane, High Town, Hereford, in 1615

Major Domo Doteall, the ancient wag of Kenchester

George Maynard, the agile youth of Hereford, surnamed the dancing devil of the city

John Oldton, a country man

Marion Mude, the widow of Stoke and beloved by Sydney

Nelly Holdfast, the pretty girl of Allensmore, and

Dame Griselda, the old woman of Ross.

The scenes in the play, newly painted by Mr. Gill 'from actual views taken on the spot', included 'the haunted gallery of the Old House'; a moonlit setting on the banks of the Wye with Lord Scudamore and the Black Friar; Hom Lacy House; a baronial hall, and the sudden appearance of a mysterious stranger 'effected by a new and ingenious contrivance'; the Dungeon of Credenhill and subterranean passage; and finally 'the mystery unrolled of the Legend of Hereford'—though what this was is not indicated, and the play now appears lost.

By now the theatre was falling on hard times. *Lascelles Directory* of 1851 poured scorn on it, describing it as 'a remarkably small and ill-supported erection', in complete contrast to the description in the *Hereford Guide* of 1827, which noted that 'the Theatre is a neat modern building and well adapted for the place'. In 1857 *Cassey's Directory* was equally contemptuous, noting that the theatre was 'extremely small and ill-supported, having a very inconvenient entrance'. The rapid turnover of management continued, and in 1853 Miss Falkland replaced Poole and Charles, only to be replaced herself in the following year by W. Peters. Nevertheless, the theatre on occasion still attracted some of the better-known touring companies, such as the Grand English Opera Company, which performed there in 1856.

A proposal was put forward in February 1857, and quickly approved, to replace the Theatre Royal with a corn exchange. The cost of the purchase and the rebuilding was £4,500, of which £2,500 was subscribed for the purchase of the site, and a further sum of £2,000 raised by ten debentures of £200 each. The property was sold by William Bosley, an innkeeper who was by then the owner, to a board of trustees, on the condition that the new building was for ever maintained as a corn exchange. On Friday, 20 March 1857, the theatre saw its last performance—the comedy *London Assurance,* and a farce, *An Object of Interest*—by desire of the committee of the Broad Street Toll-Free Corn Exchange.

Chapter IX
Inns, Taverns and Coffee Rooms

Inns and taverns, and their yards, barns and 'long rooms' or 'great rooms', have been used for a wide variety of entertainments over the years, though records are scanty. The travelling players of the 16th and early 17th centuries usually performed in inn yards, and later on many of the theatres in the county were fitted up in the barns or long rooms of inns. The regulars of some taverns, certainly in Hereford and Leominster, and probably in other towns too, formed themselves on occasion into clubs of all kinds.

In Hereford, Broad Street seems to have been a veritable entertainment quarter, its taverns used for a wide variety of exhibitions and shows. The Swan and Falcon, where Roger Kemble's company performed during their visits to the city (before moving across the street to the Half Moon), on 5 December 1774 was exhibiting 'the amazing Corsican Fairy' Maria Teresa, said to be only 34 inches high and to weigh only 26 pounds. 'Possessed of a great deal of vivacity and spirit,' the announcement claimed, 'she can speak French and Italian and gives the inquisitive mind much agreeable entertainment'. She could even dance her own country jig. At a later date the Rummer Tavern, in Bewell Street, was exhibiting a certain Mr. Ledgewood, who had been 'born without hands or arms, and with only one leg and foot'; he would 'in the acquirements of Art and Education, display various specimens of his ingenuity'.

The Swan and Falcon, which jutted out inconveniently into Broad Street, was demolished in 1790 and replaced in 1793 by the City Arms Hotel. Often known simply as the Hotel, the City Arms had a large assembly room, 70ft. long and 28ft. high., used for events of many kinds. On 14 October 1795 it was the scene for a fencing display by the Chevalière d'Eon, a 68-year-old French aristocrat who was living in England. The Chevalière was thrusting and parrying with great agility against 'an English gentleman, a professor in the art of fencing ... her

The City Arms, Broad Street, Hereford

whole deportment manifesting a philosophical indifference to her cruel reverses of fortune'. The Chevalière was in fact a much stranger character than first appears. She was touring the country giving fencing demonstrations dressed sometimes in the uniform of a captain of dragoons. During one performance in Cork, her wig fell off as she removed her helmet to reveal a bald head. She was in fact a man, who as the Chevalier D'Eon had been a distinguished diplomat, soldier and spy. After years of argument over his sex, during which large sums of money had been wagered, he had since 1777 been living as a woman.

The assembly room of the City Arms was also the scene on 23 February 1816 for John Crisp's public dinner to mark the centenary of Garrick's birth. In 1833 it was used for classes in French dancing, and in 1844 for a show by Mr. Barnardo Eagle, 'the Royal Wizard of the South', who brought his 'palace of Necromancy, or scenes of fairy land.' According to his announcement, 'the new laboratory which he intends bringing to Hereford will be more than admired by the lovers of science and recreative philosophy'.

The great room at the Mitre Tavern in Broad Street, (until recently the offices of Knight Frank), was also used for entertainments, lectures and exhibitions, such as a display of waxworks of the royal families of England and France (in 1795), and an exhibition of musical clocks from Germany (in 1796). In 1815 the great room was used by a teacher of mnemonics, Mr. Sims, who conducted lessons and examinations there, and in 1817 a concert was given by the one-man military band of Signor Rivolta. The patrons of the theatre and of the tavern, just a stone's throw apart on opposite sides of Broad Street, must have been on good terms

The Mitre, Broad Street, Hereford (Derek Foxton Collection)

with each other. In 1798 the gentlemen of the Mitre Tavern patronised a performance at the theatre of Macklin's *Man of the World*. In 1831 Charles Crisp, on his retirement as manager of the theatre, briefly became the landlord of the Mitre, and held a housewarming dinner there on Easter Monday, 4 April 1831, to return thanks 'to his friends in the city of Hereford, to Commercial Gentlemen, and to the Public generally' for their support and patronage; Sir John Cotterell was in the chair, and tickets were a sovereign each.

Some of the clubs which patronised the Hereford Theatre were based at the New Inn in Widemarsh Street (the site now occupied by the MEB showrooms). There were evidently a number of these clubs; one evening, on 14 February 1791, the 'gentlemen of the New Inn Clubs' patronised a performance of *Such Things Are!* One of them was the Thursday card-club, whose members gave up their card-playing one Thursday, on 10 March 1798, to patronise a performance of *She Stoops to Conquer* at the theatre. The various other clubs which patronised the theatres in the county would probably have also been based in taverns.

Various other groups, of indeterminate purpose, also met in taverns. On 17 October 1891, the Victoria Inn in Eign Gate, Hereford, was the venue for the fourth meeting of 'Ye Jolly Bohemians'. 'An excellent elocutionary programme was gone through', said the *Hereford Journal*, 'and a very pleasant evening spent by a large company'.

A number of temporary theatres, like the Kington Theatre, were fitted up in barns or long rooms of inns. A room at the Riverside Inn at Aymestrey was so fitted up for a performance on 10 June 1830, given by a group of six, a section of the Hereford Company of Comedians who usually performed in Leominster. The evening consisted of:

MAID AND MAGPIE, OR WHICH IS THE THIEF
(*cast: Mr. Robson, Mr. Horton, Mr. Home, Mrs. Horton, Mrs. Robson, and Mr. Jones*)

At the end of the play – a song, *I'll Never Get Married Again*,
by Mr. and Mrs. Robson
A favourite Scotch lilt, by Mr. Home
A song by Mrs. Robson
An original address by Mr. Horton called *British Tars Triumphant*, by Mr. Horton
The celebrated comic song *Bartholemew Fair*, with imitations, by Mr. Home

After which the laughable farce of
FORTUNE'S FROLIC
Or The Ploughman Turned Lord

Robin Roughhead	Mr. Robson
Rattle	Mr. Home
Old Snacks	Mr. Horton

In the character of Rattle Mr. Home will introduce the comic song of
The Beautiful Incomparable, or Rhymes in Plenty

The whole to conclude with a brilliant display of variegated Fire-Works

A room in the Lion Inn at Leintwardine was fitted up as a theatre in 1840 by the manager of the Ludlow Theatre, Mr. Henderson. It opened on 23 September for the comedy *Nabob for an Hour, or Uncle or no Uncle*, followed by a song and interlude called *A Day after the Wedding, or A Wife's First Lesson*, and concluding with a comedietta, *Mischief Making, or a French Washerwoman*; tickets were 2s. for the front seats and 1s. for those at the rear. The following month saw another play, put in 'by desire of and under the patronage of the Bachelors of Leintwardine and its vicinity', called *Honeymoon, or How to Rule a Wife*, followed by an afterpiece, *Popping*

The Riverside Inn, Aymestrey

the Question. In 1842 another play, *Catherine and Petruchio,* was performed by desire of T. Ackers Esq.; this time the actors were a section of Mr. Saunders's company, who performed at Kington, and occasionally Ledbury.

It might have been one of the more questionable strolling companies, or perhaps simply a group of villagers, who performed an evidently rather bawdy comedy in Ewyas Harold in about 1795, the announcement for which has been preserved. It begins: 'This is to give notice to all Gentlemen, ladies and others, for the diversion of the neighbouring Gentry, at Argus's Long Room in Ewyas Harold. Upon the first Monday in the new year will be performed a comedy called "The Old Doctor" or "The Antiquated Cuckold Unmask'd"… Price 2d. or 6d. the pit, 1s. the boxes each. At which time all virgins in Ewyas Harold from 15 to 25 shall be entitled to each a ticket (*gratis*) provided they prove their virginity. To begin precisely at seven o'clock in the evening'. Argus's Long Room no longer exists, but it was probably a room behind what is now the Temple Bar Inn. Like most theatres of the time it was fitted up with boxes, probably only rudimentary partitions. The cast of the play included Thomas Chandler, Mrs. Lettice Savage, and her daughter Miss Savage.

Great rooms or assembly rooms, attached either to taverns or to coffee rooms, were quite often used not for plays but for one-man performances of various kinds. These can broadly be divided into two categories, the first of which one might call performances by lecturers, magicians and conjurers. In August 1794 a gentleman calling himself Dr. Katterfeltro, M.D., F.R.S. came to Hereford, and gave demonstrations at the theatre, and at Preece's Coffee Room, of his inventions: a solar microscope, a strong magnet—which he demonstrated by using it to lift black cats up in the air—a perpetual motion machine, a fire machine, a tincture for the toothache, and sundry others. In a similar vein was a show entitled Breslaw's Capital Deceptions and Experiments, given in the same room in April 1796. Some of these performers would go on to other towns after finishing in Hereford. In

The King's Head, Ross

Ross shows sometimes took place in the assembly room at the King's Head, and it was here that Mr. Ingleby, 'the Emperor of all Conjurers', gave a show in 1815, after performing at the Hereford Theatre. His Hereford performance included a demonstration of 'the real method of cutting off a Gentleman's Head', as well as the swallowing of a dozen knives and forks, and he flattered himself—so the announcement states—that his performance would 'make amends for the many wretched attempts made lately by people professing his line'.

Secondly came shows given by comedians. On 4 July 1789 Harding's Coffee Room in Hereford, (formerly known as Woodcock's, in Milk Lane, itself now St. John Street), was the venue for Mr. Collins' Evening Brush 'for rubbing off the rust of care, and smoothing the wrinkles of melancholy'. This was an amusing mixture of music and poetry, 'punctuated with imitations of the most famous stage personalities of the time'. The show included sketches of a Yorkshire senator making an important motion for mending a window pane, a Somerset collier describing a country christening, a highlander declaiming on elocution, a Welsh exciseman reading Cato, and an Irish pastor exhorting his flock. In a similar vein were the performances given by the comedian Lee Lewes, who in 1801 also appeared at Harding's.

In Ledbury the Large Room at the George Inn, New Street, was used occasionally for comic entertainments in a similar vein, such as a performance in 1830 in which a versatile actress, Miss M.H. Carr, played 14 different characters.

CHAPTER X
Amateur Dramatics & Penny Readings

In the early 19th century enthusiastic amateurs would now and again perform at the Hereford Theatre alongside the professional cast. The amateur actors of Hereford seem to have become a little more organised by 1833, when *The Castle Spectre* was performed at the theatre by a group described as 'the City Amateurs'. This performance, undertaken by desire of the Palladian Lodge of Free Masons and with much of the entertainment relating to freemasonry, was a benefit for George Shuter, a member of the company and a freemason himself. Charles Crisp, the former manager, was a freemason too (he had retired in 1831), and evidently this early amateur group was closely connected with freemasonry. In Kington, too, amateur performances were staged now and again in this period. In 1835 the assembly room at the Swan was fitted up as a theatre for an amateur performance of *The Cricketters, or How to Play a New Game of Cricket*; the characters here included Mr. Putty, Mr. Glazier, Jimmy Cricket, Trembling George, and Swearall (the informer). This play was a burlesque based on recent events in Kington during which the cricket team had trespassed upon land owned by Messrs. Pritchard and Baynham (alias Messrs. Putty and Glazier), who had threatened the cricketers with prosecution.

Private theatricals were a fashionable diversion in country houses. At Stoke Edith they were organised into the Stoke Edith Theatricals, but often they took place in a much less organised fashion, as the first part of an evening's entertainment, before dinner and dancing. One amusing example of these informal private theatricals is a performance at Cowarne Court, home of the Bourne family, in 1889. The play was *Romeo and Juliet, or the Shamming of the True, an Atrocious Outrage in Five Acts*. The handwritten programme gives the cast as 'Capulet, President of the Verona Reform League'; 'Romeo, a Conservative and a Gentleman'; 'Mercutio, a Gentleman and a Conservative' (played by Count Lubienski-

Bodenham, of Rotherwas); 'Friar Lawrence, a ghostly father'; and 'Juliet, the Girl of the Period'. F.C. Kempson was stage manager. Ruth Bourne's unpublished diary describes the evening as follows: 'At eight thirty the company arrived and at nine Romeo and Juliet was begun. It went off with great go. The servants on the stairs were very appreciative and clapped and encored everything. I got through my part without a hitch. Supper was at eleven, and dancing went on till nearly two. Enjoyed the evening very much … Faith did Juliet very well. She talked in a short sharp impertinent way. Her hair was frizzed in a vulgar fashion'.

From the 1860s amateur theatricals started to gain a wider popularity, and numerous often short-lived societies were formed. One of these was the Ross Amateur Association, which gave annual performances in the Corn Exchange in Ross. A review of an 1875 performance adjudged that 'their performers acquitted themselves with the credibility usually to be found in a provincial company of amateurs; the acting of Mr. H.G. Treasure, Mr. Counsell and Mr. Keyworth, as a low comedian, being somewhat above the normal character', but, it went on, no doubt they would get better, and their elocution improve, when their shyness had worn off. The leading light of the association was John Counsell, billed in the *Hereford Journal* as 'the Theatrical "Man of Ross"'. In an entertainment at the Forester's Hall in Hereford in February 1882, John Counsell was joined by members of the Monmouth Histrionic Club and the Hereford Amateur Dramatic Society, as well as the Ross Amateur Association. During the 1880s Counsell organised annual theatricals at the Corn Exchange in Ross. The Hereford Amateur Dramatic Society was founded in April 1874. Closely connected with the city companies of the Hereford Rifle Volunteers, it held a performance of *The Rivals* at the Shirehall in 1875, in which the stage manager was Sergeant Hatton, and Sir Anthony Absolute was played by Private John Hatton. Tickets for this performance were expensive, with reserved seats costing 5s.

The Kington Amateur Dramatic Society was founded in the 1860s, and in 1865 performed an entertainment at the Prince of Wales' Theatre at Burton Hall in Kington. With Queen Victoria as its patroness, this club evidently had considerable social cachet, and the

A. A.

ROSS CORN EXCHANGE.

FOR TWO NIGHTS,

THURSDAY and FRIDAY, OCTOBER 28 and 29.

THE Members of the ROSS AMATEUR ASSOCIATION will give TWO DRAMATIC PERFORMANCES on the above dates.

NEW SCENERY!

NEW MUSIC!

The Performance will commence each evening with J. B. Johnstone's celebrated Drama, in two Acts, entitled

BEN BOLT;

OR, THE WRECK OF THE ALICE!

Programme of Scenery.

ACT I.— MORNING.

Oh! don't you remember the school, Ben Bolt,
And the master so kind and so true,
And the sweet little nook by the clear running brook,
Where we gather'd the flowers as they grew?

THE MILL, SCHOOL-HOUSE, AND CHURCH, On the Beach of Rock Head Ferry.

ACT II.—NIGHT.

The mill has gone to decay, Ben Bolt,
And quiet now reigns all around:
And the old rustic porch, with its roses so sweet,
Lies scattered and fall'n to the ground.

DILAPIDATED SCHOOL-HOUSE & ROOFLESS MILL.

" The churchyard and slab of granite so grey."

Concluding on Thursday evening with a Laughable Farce, in one Act, by Lenox Horne, Esq., entitled

TWO HEADS ARE BETTER THAN ONE.

On Friday evening, the Performance will conclude with a Screaming Farce, in one Act, by Thomas J. Williams, Esq., entitled

DANDELION'S DODGES.

The Members have much pleasure in informing the public that they have (at great expense) secured the services of the celebrated

MISS ANNIE RICHARDSON (from the Theatre Royal, Haymarket).

For full particulars, see Programmes, 1d. each.

ADMISSION (by Ticket only)—Stalls (numbered and reserved), 2s.; Second Seats, 1s.; Promenade, 6d. A plan of the room may be seen and stalls secured at Mr. Powle's, Stationer. Other Tickets at the various Booksellers. Doors open at 7.30; curtain to rise at 8 precisely. Carriages for 10.15.

Conductor of the Orchestra .... Mr. J. Squire.
Acting Manager.......... Mr. H. G. Treasure.
Stage Manager ...... Mr. John A. J. Counsell.

An advertisement for a performance by the Ross Amateur Association in 1869

Kington Amateur Dramatic Club.

WEDNESDAY & THURSDAY, DEC. 7 & 8, 1881.

CASTE

Under the Patronage of

RIGHT HON. LORD ORMATHWAITE.
EDWARD BACON, ESQ.
REV. COULSON BRIDGES.
REV. W. H. BRADLEY.
B. BODENHAM, ESQ.
COLONEL DALLAS.
REV. JAMES DAVIES.
H. P. DAVIES, ESQ.
E. DELFOSSE, ESQ.
F. L. EVELYN, ESQ.
E. H. GREENLY, ESQ.
R. GREEN, ESQ.
REV. C. E. MADDISON GREEN.
G. FOOTE, ESQ.
CAPTAIN JAMES.
CAPTAIN OTWAY.
MAJOR D. PEPLOE PEPLOE.
B. PHILPIN, ESQ.
SIR RICHARD GREEN PRICE.
COLONEL PRICE.
W. F. TAYLOR, ESQ.
ANTHONY TEMPLE, ESQ.
F. R. TIDD PRATT, ESQ.
MAJOR W. WORSLEY WORSWICK.
REV. M. WOOD.

597·A

Registered.

R. W. SATCHELL, Printer, Kington.

BURTON HALL, KINGTON.

PROGRAMME OF
AMATEUR DRAMATIC PERFORMANCE

To be given on THURSDAY & FRIDAY, APRIL 5th & 6th.

In aid of the funds of the Kington Company
1st H.R. Volunteers.

"THE OLD STORY,"

An original Comedy, by H. J. Byron, Esq.

Waverly Brown (*Bachelor*)	Mr. ALFRED PARKER	Mrs. Minerva Deadset (*Widow*) Mrs. R. WILLIAMS
Thomson (*from Toots*)	Mr. T. EDWARDS	Miss Snipely (*Spinster*) Miss MALKIN
P. N. Jones (*Poet*)	Mr. E. C. ROSSITER	Miss Crichett (*Spinster*) Miss DREW
Captain Kinton (*unattached*)	Mr. E. F. MITCHELL	Lucy Brown (*Brown's Niece*) Miss MARION MITCHELL
Wilkinson (*Servant*)	Mr. W. H. STANWAY	Fritters (*her Maid*) Miss DAVIS

ACT I.
SCENE—Interior of a Country Cottage Ornee.
ACT II.
The same.
Six weeks are supposed to have elapsed between the First and Second Act.

"THE LOAN OF A LOVER,"

Musical Comedietta by J. R. Planché, Esq.

Captain Amersfort	Mr. E. F. MITCHELL	Delve Mr. J. FRYER
Peter Spyk	Mr A. PARKER	Gertrude Miss EDITH MITCHELL
Swyzel	Mr A. J. DILLOW	Ernestine Rosendaal Mrs. R. WILLIAMS

SCENE—Garden of a Villa near Utrecht.

The whole of the Scenery is painted specially for this representation by W. T. HEMSLEY, Esq.,
of the Grand Theatre, London.

Musical arrangements under the management of Mrs. CHARLESWORTH & Miss. MITCHELL.

Stage Manager—Mr. T. E. PARKER.   Acting Manager—Mr. H. F. MEREDITH.

Amateur Theatricals in Kington, 1888

review commented that the front rows were 'filled with a fashionable array of the gentry'. But not content with just an amateur dramatic society, Kington also boasted a flourishing amateur minstrel society, founded in the 1850s as the Ethiopian Serenaders. It had over 50 performers who sang 'refined and funny songs, pathetic ballads and choruses, charming plantation songs and brilliant witticisms'.

The village of Kingsland also had a flourishing amateur dramatic society. It was founded in 1880, when a series of entertainments was being organised in the village to raise money for the poor of the parish. A certain Philip Turner, from Eardisland, was asked to recite a poem, but by way of a change he suggested theatricals, and the first of many productions was Gilbert & Sullivan's *Box and Cox*. Most of the performances took place at the Large Room at the Croase, the upper floor of a large barn at the Croase House in Kingsland; this made an attractive little theatre, but its thatched roof, uneven floor and difficult stairs made it somewhat of a potential fire risk. The performances were popular, and at one of them 500 people tried to gain admission.

The principal amateur performers in Kingsland were people such as the local doctor, who often took women's parts, the rector's wife, and the

91

Kingsland Amateur Dramatic Society

AN

ENTERTAINMENT

Will be given by the above, assisted by

Mr. HARRY DAVIS & Mr. FULLER,

IN

The Corn Exchange Hall, Leominster,

ON

Monday, May the 7th, 1888,

IN AID OF THE

Leominster Football Club.

Under the following distinguished patronage.

Arkwright, J. H., Esq.	Grey, Rev. J. C.
Ashton, Major,	Gammidge, W. N., Esq.
Andrews, C. D., Esq.,	Horton, Rev. R.
Barnett, S. Esq.,	Hyde, W. E., Esq,,
Baillie, Rev. T. G.	Heygate, Major,
Blundell, Edwin, Esq.,	Heygate, Robert, Esq.,
Bowen, E. P., Esq.,	Lane, T. W., Esq.,
Buss, H. D., Esq.,	Lucas, E. S., Esq.,
Bentley, Rev. R.,	Powlett, Rev. E. O.
Barneby, W. H., Esq.,	Peppercorn, Rev. A. T.,
Benn, C. A., Esq.,	Rankin, J., Esq., M.P.,
Boyce, W. S., Esq.,	Rogers, Rev. Father,
Clowes, J., Esq.,	Reece, T., Esq.(Birmingham)
Davis, J. J., Esq.,	Sale, W. T., Esq.,
Davies, Rev. H. R.,	Stallard, T. B., Esq.,
Dunne, T. R., Esq.,	Southern, E. W., Esq.,
Edwards, O., Esq.,	Southall, H. J., Esq.,
Gunnell, Capt. E. V.,	Thomas, A. W., Esq.,
Gregg, Edwin, Esq.,	Woodhouse, R. H., Esq.,

Williams, H. S., Esq.

Admission :—Reserved Seats 2s ; Second Seats 1s ; Promenade (limited) 6d. Balcony (Front Row Reserved) 2s ; Promenade 1s.

Tickets and Plan of Room at Mr. C. J. Saxby's.

DOORS OPEN AT ·7, TO COMMENCE AT 7.30.

Carriages may be ordered for 10.30.

Mr. Mayor's Band will be in attendance.

SAXBY, TYP., LEOMINSTER.

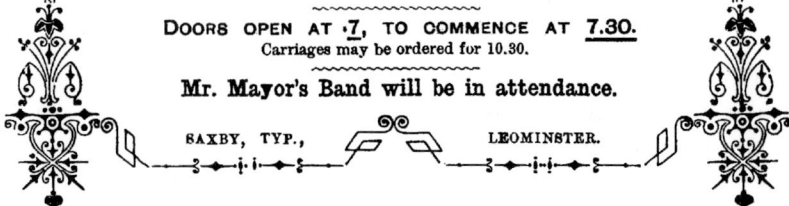

The first floor of the barn at the Croase used by Kingsland's
amateur dramatic and minstrel societies. The curve of the proscenium arch can
just be made out below and beyond the second the two main roof trusses

bank manager from Kington. Their performances raised money for a wide variety of causes, from the poor of the parish, and the village school, to a new fire engine. Kingsland too had its own minstrel society, which also gave performances at the Croase.

In Ledbury the United Service Dramatic Club flourished in the 1860s, under the management of Captain Disney Roebuck, formerly of the Royal Welch Fusiliers. In December 1869 Captain Roebuck's club performed *East Lynne* at the Feathers Hotel in Ledbury, and in the following year *Bread Sauce on the First of September*; audiences for this, however, were sadly sparse.

This was also the age when penny readings became popular. A 'counter-attraction to the tavern' (as the Fownhope penny readings were described), they generally consisted of a series of readings from novels or poetry alternating with songs and duets. They appear to have been highly popular; in Ross, where the readings took place in the Corn Exchange, one of the first meetings attracted 560 people. The proceeds of the evening were usually given to worthy charitable causes such as, in Ross in 1867, the Ross Mental Improvement Society. Penny readings were held not just in the major towns but in a lot of villages—Colwall, Whitchurch,

Fownhope, Goodrich, Much Marcle and Dilwyn among them; in Much Marcle the readings sometimes attracted over 400 people. In Ledbury, however, the audience was apparently less respectful of these attempts to instill culture, a portion of them either misbehaving so that it was difficult to hear the performers, or clapping 'with more gusto than is commendable'. In Hereford readings were given in the Corn Exchange, but there seems to have been little interest. Readings and songs of this kind were sometimes held in workhouses, in a worthy effort to bring culture to the poor.

CHAPTER XI
Music Hall Artistes & other Entertainers

The Hereford Theatre may have been replaced by the Corn Exchange in 1857, but Mr. Peters, the last manager of the theatre, remained as manager of its replacement, which was licensed to seat up to 500 people. In addition Hereford had the Shirehall, built in 1819, which could hold an audience of up to 1,000.

Some of the most popular shows in the 1850s were given by comedians following in the tradition of the very popular Charles Mathews, with his impersonations of a bewildering succession of different characters. The *Hereford Times* wrote in 1859 that 'no kind of public entertainment is so popular as the running monologue, displaying a succession of characters personated by the same individual. It admits of the introduction of an inexhaustible fund of anecdote and incident'.

One of the most celebrated comedians of the 1850s was W.S. Woodin, with his 'Olio of Oddities' (an 'Olio' meaning a mixture) subtitled 'an original mimical, metrical, and polygraphic entertainment, illustrated by nearly 100 instantaneous metamorphoses of voice, character, and costume'. The *Hereford Times* wrote that:

CORN EXCHANGE, ROSS.

FOR ONE NIGHT ONLY !!
FRIDAY, APRIL 26th.
Doors open at half-past 7 ; commence at 8.
First Seats, 2s. ; Second Seats, 1s. ; Back Seats, 6d.
Tickets to be had at the *Gazette* Office.

W. S. WOODIN,
From the Polygraphic Hall, London,
In his Laughable Sketches of the Visitors at

BADEN BADEN,
Including
HIGH LIFE !! COMICAL INCIDENTS !!
LOW LIFE !!
MARVELLOUS TRANSFORMATIONS !!
FAST LIFE !! SONGS !! DANCES !! &c., &c.
Also in a SINGLE-HANDED Farce, entitled

UP IN THE AIR !!
In the course of which Mr. Woodin appears out of windows, doors, up ladders, and over parapets almost simultaneously ! ! ! ! ! !   Angelina reading her love-letter on the leads amidst peals of laughter, Young Men, Old Ladies, Irishman, Scotchman, Thief, Police, &c. The amusing plot which runs through this piece, the rapidity and completeness of the metamophosis, &c., the novel and original character of the monologue have rendered this the most successful Entertainment that Mr. Woodin has ever presented to the Public.

A notice of W.S. Woodin performing in Ross in 1867

95

The species of monopolylogue entertainment which the elder Mathews made popular ... has had no smarter or more versatile professor than the young gentleman who, a few years ago, opened his 'Carpet-Bag' for the delectation of the London sight-seers. Changing the title and, in some measure, the character of his entertainment, as he grew in favour with metropolitan audiences, Mr. Woodin has for successive 'seasons' combined in his 'Olio of Oddities' a mélange of humorous eccentricities, having more or less of bearing upon the fashions, the popularities, or the foibles of the day. By dint of great power of face, extraordinary flexibility of voice, and miraculous changes of costume, he has contrived to present a varied series of performances, which have established themselves as among the standard amusements of London. During the fashionable 'recess' he is making, after the fashion of stars of his magnitude, a provincial tour, and takes Hereford in his eccentric orbit.

On 22 and 23 January 1858 Woodin performed his Olio in the assembly room of the Green Dragon Hotel in Hereford; from Hereford he went on Leominster, performing in the Town Hall on 25 January. The *Hereford Times* was enthusiastic in its praise:

His 'trip by the train' comprises the work of a whole company of players; he personifies almost simultaneously an immense variety of passengers and attendants, young, middle aged and old, male and female, timid, querulous and debonnair, and it is not only that the momentary duck of his head below the elevated flap of his table is sufficient to transmogrify him into altogether another person from the one you were the instant before looking at, but without disappearing at all he changes voice and style, and visage and toilet, so as to realise the idea of half a dozen different persons almost at the same time. Perhaps the supernaculum of the performances was the impersonation of 'Miss Clara Chatterway', the fashionable young lady. The make up was marvellous. The decoleté style of feminine evening costume, with its prominent display of artificial appliance, the cloud of crinoline, the mass of elaborated hair – of course in deference to the prevailing mode, of the favourite Eugenie-tint – were the perfection of mocking imitation, nor were the carriage and deportment, the finnicking with gloves and handkerchief, the complicated operation at the piano, less perfect in their way a caricature, but not a burlesque or vulgarity; in short the transcript to an incredible degree of realisation of a remarkably fine woman dressed *à la merveille*.

Advertisement for an olio evening in Hereford,
and a notice of performances in Leominster
in 1789

This was the first of many visits Woodin paid to Herefordshire in the 1850s and 60s—performing at the Green Dragon, and later the Corn Exchange, in Hereford, at the Town Hall in Leominster (or the Corn Exchange, built in 1859), at Milner's Public Hall in Kington, and at the Corn Exchange in Ross (built in 1862, burnt down in 1939). After the success of his 'Olio of Oddities', Woodin made provincial tours with other shows such as 'Baden Baden', 'Elopement Extraordinary' and 'Bachelor's Box'.

Singing was not Woodin's strong point, the *Hereford Times* admitting that 'as a vocalist, Mr. Woodin's powers are not great'. In this regard he was overshadowed by Mr. and Mrs. Howard Paul, who performed their 'Patchwork' at the Town Hall in Leominster on 25 May 1858, followed by two performances at the Shirehall in Hereford, as part of a tour following a highly successful season at the Adelphi in London. 'Among the unconnected shreds and patches will be found 14 impersonations of character; Scotch,

English and Irish ballads, operatic selections, whims and oddities. The whole forming an agreeable mélange of melody and merriment'. The *Hereford Times* reprinted an enthusiastic review from the *Glasgow Herald*:

> The characters [Patchwork] embraces are about equal in number to those of an ordinary play, and the novelty is that the entire dramatis personae are sustained by only two persons. So complete and finished are their rapidly executed changes of habilment, accent and gait that many of the audience, were they not previously and purposely apprised of it, could not detect the same person in any two of the diverse characters reproduced. Mrs. Paul's appearances are good studies ... Whether as the haughty and aristocratic young lady, the talkative and implacable wife, the uninitiated but warm-hearted Irish nurse, the quaintly attired but querulous Newhaven fishwife, the smiling and luxurious Spanish maiden, or the tender and peaceful Aurelia, she is alike consistently characteristic and true to nature's copy ... Her voice, although properly of the contralto order, partakes of the diversity which is the striking feature of her other parts, and is sweetly clear as well as full-bodied and sonorous.

Another couple specialising in these running monologues with their scores of different characters were Mr. and Mrs. Charles Cotton, who came to Hereford with their show 'The Rose, Thistle and Shamrock' in March 1859:

> Tim Raggerty, an Irish ballad singer with lots of blarney, Mr. Christopher Squib, an exaggerated 'swell' with an overplus of hair and assurance, and a country bumpkin, with a great deal of droll singing and acting, are among the best characters. In the latter of them he improvised a set of doggerel hexamaters, ingeniously hitting off the sporting events of the day.

Just as popular as these running monologues and the many ventriloquism shows in a similar vein were the shows, or séances, given by illusionists and magicians, reflecting a widespread interest in spiritualism and in the fashionable techniques of mesmerism and hypnotism. Among those coming to Hereford were the Misses Anderson, daughters of Professor Anderson, the 'Wizard of the North'; during their show at the Corn Exchange one of the sisters was mesmerised, blindfolded, and asked to identify items belonging to members of the audience. She guessed correctly every time.

By 1875 many shows of this kind were advertised as exposés of the more run-of-the-mill conjuring shows, together with demonstrations of the real thing. In March 1875 Dr. Monk came to the Hereford Corn Exchange to give two 'lecture-séances', billed as an 'exposé of the so-called marvellous tricks of modern conjurers, which are falsely alleged to be identical with the phenomena of spiritualism'. Popular conjuring tricks such as messages from spirits, blood-writing on the arm, and the way in which conjurers appeared to float freely in the air without visible support, were explained away. The audience were instructed how to detect tricks of this sort, and then directed how to form spirit circles so as to elicit real spirit manifestations in their own homes.

Another genre highly popular from the 1850s onwards were the minstrel shows, or 'Ethiopian entertainments'. The most famous minstrel band, Christy's Minstrels, rarely left London, but they had many imitators. Minstrels, comedians and magicians aside, the corn exchanges of the county were also used by a wide variety of music hall performers, such as Horace Chester—'the Merry Monologuist', and (in Hereford) Bugler Carr, who travelled the music halls with an act part of which apparently involved balancing a copy of the *Hereford Times* on his nose, setting fire to it, and still balancing the charred paper. In a more solemn vein, the Ross Corn Exchange was used in 1867 for a temperance lecture given by George King, a converted pugilist, (the announcement pointedly headed 'To the Working Men of Ross').

An evening of both ventriloquism and minstrel songs at the Corn Exchange, Hereford, in 1867

99

The Newmarket Tavern. The old theatre is a single storey wing with arched windows on the left of the building

In February 1859 advertisements started to appear for a theatre at the new Hereford Cattle Market, in an annex to the Cattle Market Tavern (now the Newmarket Tavern). In 1852 the room had been described (in *Slater's* directory) as a music hall. The *Hereford Times* announced:

> The Gentry and residents of Hereford and the vicinity are respect-
> fully informed that the above establishment is open every evening
> (Wednesday excepted) by the Brecon Company, whose excellence
> has been recognised by the elite of the county during the past three
> months.

Under the management of George Bolton, the theatre stayed open for race nights and the steeplechase week in March. 'The excellent selection of pieces to be performed', said the *Hereford Times,* 'will doubtless attract a fair complement of pleasure-seekers to witness the clever representations of Mr. Bolton's *corps dramatique*'. The season's performances included the melodrama *Black-Eyed Susan,* and the farce *Betsy Baker.* Two years later, in 1861, the theatre opened, rather incongruously, as the Theatre Royal. *The Hereford Journal* announced on 20 February that:

> The Cattle Market Tavern is now fitted up for farce and
> pantomime, and it presents [*sic*] nightly thronged audiences to
> witness the performance of a company of dramatists led by Mr.
> Egerton.

Fred Egerton, the new manager, staged a new Christmas pantomime, 'pronounced by the press and public of Gloucester and Swansea to be the best ever produced', entitled *Puck and Robin Goodfellow*. Tickets cost 2s. for reserved seats, 1s. for the pit, and 6d. for the gallery. Despite its grand new name, however, the theatre did not thrive; its advertisements soon petered out, and in 1866 the building was known as a 'concert room'. It is now the modest function room of the Newmarket Tavern.

Ten years after the old Hereford Theatre was pulled down to be replaced by the Corn Exchange, the city acquired another music hall. The Alhambra Music Hall and Palace of Amusement, which opened in September 1867, was situated just off Bridge Street, at the rear of the Royal Oak Inn. It was an attractive building; around three sides of the hall, with its coved ceiling, was a balcony with ornamental balustrading, supported on wooden columns; the balcony was reached by an ornamental staircase at the back of the hall. At least to begin with, the Alhambra opened every night, with an entire change of performance twice a week. Tickets were cheap: 1s. for the stalls, 6d. for the balcony and upper tier of boxes, and 3d. for the body of the hall. Probably because the proprietor, Charles Testo, used playbills for advertising, there is little record of what entertainment was provided. For a few weeks after the

The interior of the Alhambra at the end of its days in the 1930s
(Derek Foxton Collection)

opening, though, Testo placed announcements in the *Hereford Journal*: on 16 September Mademoiselle Bertha Purcell and Mr. F. Addison from the Royal English Opera performed for a few nights, and on 5 October Miss Annie Anderson, 'the great serio-comic characteristic vocalist' was re-engaged for six nights.

The Alhambra, however, does not appear to have been a success as a music hall, despite its cheap seats. Performers went instead to the Corn Exchange, which seated many more. Instead, the Alhambra was used for other purposes; according to the *Hereford Times*, it 'had a short reign of success at a time when the penny readings and the spelling bee were popular forms of entertainment'. Apparently one of the lady proof-readers at the *Hereford Times* did particularly well at the spelling bee contests. In a directory of 1876-77 the building was referred to as a lecture hall: 'a spacious room, well fitted up, capable of seating about 700 persons', and even though many smaller

ALHAMBRA MUSIC HALL, HEREFORD.

CHARLES TESTO takes this medium of communicating with his friends and the public to inform them that he OPENS, THE ABOVE PLACE OF AMUSEMENT on MONDAY, SEPTEMBER 2nd, and he assures them that it is his determination to conduct the same on the strictest principles of respectability, combined with first-class talent. He trusts to receive their kind support. For programme of entertainment see Day Bills.

Notice of the opening of the Alhambra placed in the Hereford Journal *on 31 August 1867, and, below, on 14 September thanking people for their support and announcing a forthcoming event, with items at the Corn Exchange beneath*

Public Notices.

ALHAMBRA MUSIC HALL, HEREFORD.
Proprietor : CHARLES TESTO.

C. T. takes this opportunity of thanking his patrons for the liberal support bestowed upon him since the opening of the above Hall, and begs respectfully to inform them that, in addition to the present powerful Company, he has engaged for a few nights the services of those highly gifted and celebrated Artistes, Mademoiselle BERTHA PURCELL and Mr. F. ADDISON from the Royal English Opera, London, who will make their first appearance on MONDAY EVENING, September 16th. Doors open at 7 o'clock, commence at half-past. Prices of Admission : Stalls, 1s. ; Balcony and Upper Tier of Boxes, 6d. ; Body of the Hall, 3d.

HARRY CLIFTON'S ANNUAL TOUR !
CORN EXCHANGE, HEREFORD,
MONDAY, SEPTEMBER 16.

IT is respectfully announced that HARRY CLIFTON, the celebrated Comic Vocalist, will give a first-class CONCERT, on the above-named date.

ARTISTES,—

MISS FANNY EDWARDS,
MISS ANNIE KINNIARD,

MR. W. ORKINS AND CYRUS BELL,
MR. W. HALLIDAY,
MR. HARRY CLIFTON.

Doors open at half-past Seven, to commence at Eight. Front Seats, 2s. ; Second Seats, 1s. ; Back Seats, 6d. Tickets may be obtained from Mr. Jakeman and Mr. Phillips, Stationers, High Town.

music halls closed in 1878 with the imposition of stringent new safety regulations, the Alhambra remained in use until 1892. In that year it

The proposed façade for St. George's Hall, built c.1880, in Bewell Street
(Derek Foxton Collection)

finally closed its doors and became a seed warehouse, part of the premises of Messrs. Franklin Barnes. It remained in use as a warehouse for many years. In 1928 a theatrical producer from Henley-on-Thames, Cyril Wood, wrote to the *Hereford Times* with a suggestion that the old theatre, still complete, should be renovated and reopened, and offered any assistance he could, but his proposal came to nothing. In 1936 the building was demolished to provide bigger premises for Franklin Barnes. Today its site forms part of another place of entertainment in the shape of the Crystal Rooms.

Also in Hereford was St. George's Hall, situated at the west end of Bewell Street. Built in about 1880, this hall was used for the usual fare of plays, minstrel shows, and magicians—such as (in 1882) Herr Dobler, 'the Wizard of the World, in his Palace of Necromantic Gems, wonderful illusions, and magical surprises'. On one occasion the hall also provided winter quarters for a circus. Early in the following century it was turned into a skating rink during a roller-skating craze, and was used for special events such as a fancy dress carnival held there in 1911. However, the hall suffered from a structural defect, and after a

Skating at St. George's Hall in 1911

short while was declared unsuitable for public entertainment purposes; the elaborate façade which had been planned was never built (see illustration on previous page). In later years it was used by a firm of organ builders, Ingram and Company, before becoming the Hereford Motor Company's garage. After these successive turns of fortune the hall was finally destroyed in a fire in 1942.

At about the same time that St. George's Hall was being built, a Foresters' Hall (the Foresters were a form of Friendly Society), was built in Widemarsh Street; in later years it was to become the Garrick Theatre. In February 1882 the hall was used for an amateur theatrical entertainment starring John A.J. Counsell, dubbed 'the Theatrical "Man of Ross"'. The evening consisted of 'songs and character sketches, ventriloquism, a stump oration, instrumental music etc'. It started with a comedy, *Up for the Cattle Show,* in which John Counsell and his wife sang a humorous duet, 'Peter, my Pooty Lad', and concluded with a farce called *Leave It To Me (an anti-spiritualistic absurdity).* The performance was a great success; the *Hereford Journal* wrote that 'to say the audience were convulsed with laughter would convey but a slight impression of the merriment caused …'. Tickets cost 2s. for reserved seats, 1s. for second seats, and 6d. for promenade. In November 1882 the Foresters' Hall showed a panorama called 'The Pacific Railway', the Shirehall being unsuitable for 'Panoramas, or any entertainments that have scenic effects', presumably because of the fire risks from the gas-fuelled projectors.

Through the 1880s the hall was used intermittently for shows of various kinds (though it appears on an 1888 map as a drill hall), and by 1889 had its own Foresters' Hall Company of Players. In the following year, 1890, the hall was leased to Arthur Henderson, a former scene painter at Covent Garden and the Haymarket Theatre. Henderson remodelled the interior completely, turning the building into, by all accounts, a very attractive theatre. The *Hereford Journal* was lavish in its praise: 'From a structure that, though it had its uses, was little better than a huge barn, it has been so altered as to compare favourably with some of the prettiest and most attractive theatres in provincial towns'. The report described the theatre:

> At the stage end of the hall has been erected a handsome proscenium, bearing at the top a series of exquisitely executed paintings, emblematic of music and the drama in their different phases – such as tragedy, comedy and opera &c. – slightly below which is blazoned the appropriate motto 'All the World's a Stage' and a mask of Shakespeare. The walls have been admirably decorated by the lessee, and here he shows all those qualities which render his name memorable in the records of Covent Garden, the Haymarket, and the other theatres with which he has been concerned.

The Athenaeum, as Henderson called his new theatre, opened on 1 November 1890, closing temporarily later in the same month for the building of a new gallery with raked seats. This building work took about a month, and the Athenaeum reopened, now according to its publicity 'one of the cosiest little theatres in the Kingdom'. The theatre had attractive decorative plasterwork and statuary (carried out by Panicoli Pellegrino, a composition figure maker, of Bridge Street), and upholstered forms to replace the benches of the Forester's Hall. The *Hereford Journal* noted, ironically considering the building's later history, that 'every precaution which could be devised has been taken to prevent any outbreak of fire'; the walls were concrete, and coated with asbestos paint. The theatre seated 650, and had two entrances, the one nearest Newmarket Street leading to the balcony and the better auditorium seats, the second leading up a narrow passageway to the cheapest seats at the rear of the hall.

The Royal Athenaeum, as it was known from August 1891, attracted some of the best-known London productions. The Shakespearean actress Mrs. Bandmann Palmer came three times with her company, which would probably then have included the young Mrs. Patrick Campbell. Mrs. Bandmann Palmer had played the role of Hamlet to great acclaim, and on one of her visits to the Athenaeum took on the leading part in *Richard III*; but 'was hardly successful in this more masculine role', according to the *Hereford Times*. There were also popular performances by illusionists and mind-readers such as Professor Duprez, 'the Monarch of Magicians and world-famous illusionist and prestidigitator'. The

The Drill Hall forms the backdrop to a motor car rally, September 1904
(Derek Foxton Collection)

professor's sleights of hand, said the *Hereford Journal*, 'were exceedingly brilliant and fairly bewildered the audience, while his dark séance was exceedingly clever'. He also had three performing dogs which he had trained to perform tricks. Popular too at the Athenaeum were burlesques—the forerunners of musical comedy and revue—such as *Randolph the Reckless*.

In October 1894 some amateur theatricals were held at a new venue, the Drill Hall, in Friar Street, 'in aid of the Drill Hall Building Fund'. This hall, an unimposing shed-like structure with at first only a single stove for heating, was to be the drill hall for the 1st Herefordshire Rifle Volunteers, commanded by Colonel Scobie. However, it had a stage, and as a theatre it provided a larger alternative to the Athenaeum. In the following year, 1895, the D'Oyly Carte Opera Company came to the Drill Hall, as did Professor Crocker's Educated Horses—involving no less than 30 horses and donkeys on stage. The Drill Hall was also used on occasion by horse trainers, such as Norton B. Smith, 'Emperor of All Horse Trainers', who invited people to 'bring your kickers, runaways, jibbers, plungers, fighters … and man-eating stallions, and I will handle them and subdue them'.

In 1895 Henderson left the Athenaeum—or as it had come to be known, the Theatre Royal and Opera House—to be replaced by Edward

Advertisement for a performance by a Japanese troupe that included
'the first Japanese Ladies and Children ... permitted to leave that country'
in the Shirehall, Hereford, in June 1867

Shenton. Shenton continued the same mixture of visiting London companies and humorists, and in April 1895 Padey Pennington, the 'humorist, ventriloquist, mimist, thought reader and genuine hypnotist', appeared there, advertising rather impressively that 'starting from the Athenaeum at five o'clock on Monday, Mr. Pennington will find a pin hidden anywhere in Hereford'. However, managers for one reason or another did not stay long, and Shenton was replaced as resident manager by the unfortunately named Wentworth Croke. Croke himself soon left, to be replaced in April 1900 by George Wilson, and then in August by Edward Hollingshead, nephew of the famous theatre manager John Hollingshead. The Theatre Royal now advertised itself as 'the most comfortable place of amusement in Hereford', and continued to attract some of the best London companies, among them the Strand Comedy Company and the Lyceum Repertoire Company. In 1905 the Theatre Royal, now with yet another manager, Arthur Carlton, was renamed yet again, this time becoming the Garrick Theatre. It also began to show moving pictures, advertising in October 1905 an evening of 'Edison and Granville's latest electric animated pictures'.

The Drill Hall was continuing to thrive. In 1900 performances there included *Tannhaüser* by the Carl Rosa Opera Company, with a chorus of 60 on stage; *Charley's Aunt* in August; an appearance by the famous music hall artiste Albert Chevalier in September, singing a selection of his best known songs, such as 'Anky Panky', 'It Gets Me Talked Abaht', and 'Mafekin' Night'. Chevalier's tour also took him to the Market Hall in Ross. The following month, January 1901, the D'Oyly Carte Opera Company appeared at the Drill Hall in Hereford and the Market Hall in Ross.

Many of the big shows were now being put on in the Drill Hall. The Corn Exchange was also used more and more for a variety of performances, including the ever-popular minstrel shows, and shows of animated photos—such as Dyson's Diorama and Gipsy Choir. The Shirehall was often used for concerts, but in 1892 it was packed for an entertainment given by George Grossmith, author of *The Diary of a Nobody*, published the same year. Grossmith, known as 'the Society Clown', had been a member of the D'Oyly Carte Opera Company until 1889, when he started touring Britain and America as a singer and entertainer, and on this occasion the Shirehall was packed for his last show in the country before leaving for an American tour. It consisted of a humorous musical recital, the first part entitled 'Is Music a Failure?'; this included a description of a rehearsal of a new pastoral cantata by a country amateur choir, and two songs: 'Go on Talking, Don't Mind Me', and 'The Society Nigger'. The second part, entitled 'Playacting', included a song, 'The Stage and Your Stiff Relations', and sketches of 'The Forgetful Barrister', 'The Old Organ Man', 'The Up-to-Date Mamma', and 'Mr. Henry Irving on the Stage'.

Chapter XII
Menageries, Circuses & Fairs

A hundred years ago circuses were far more popular than they are today; in the 1950s, an ancient inhabitant of Much Dewchurch recalled how, when he was a boy, circuses, complete with elephants and other animals, used to process past his front door. On occasion too, one could glimpse elephants and camels being given baths in the Wye, below the Castle Green in Hereford.

The first circus to come to the county was probably Humphreys and Sanders's troop from the Royal Circus, which gave a performance in a yard in Bye Street, Hereford, in 1792. A few years later, in 1798, there was an exhibition at Worcester Races of two live kangaroos, recently brought to England from the newly discovered land of Australia. The *Hereford Journal* reported that 'the curiosity of the Nobility and Gentry and the Public in general was so much excited that they flocked in immense crowds to see those uncommon creatures, and the greatest surprise and admiration was expressed by all ranks, on viewing such wonderful quadrupeds, which differ so much in formation from all other animals that it is impossible to form a proper idea of their size and figure without seeing them'. From Worcester they came to Hereford, where they were exhibited in a large caravan in St. Owen Street, then were taken to Ross the following day. More unusual still were the Icknewmons—'worshipped by the ancient Egyptians'—the coati-mundi from Brazil, and the ursine sloth, all brought to Hereford by another circus in April 1801.

Circuses grew larger and larger. In the 1850s Wallett's Great Equestrian Company had 'the largest and most talented troupe of equestrian gymnasts, acrobats, rope dancers, pole sprinters, summersault throwers, jesters and clowns'. They performed in Leominster on 18 May 1858, Bromyard on the 19th, Hereford on the 20th (in the Cattle Market), and Ross on the 21st. The performance began with a procession which included, improbably, the state carriage of Charles II, purchased by a nobleman from the Royal Stables, as well as 40 knights in armour, preceded by a military band in ancient costume. Wallett's also included jesters who, the *Hereford Times* thought, were 'only as far inferior to the declamation of the legitimate stage as they were superior to the vulgar feebleness that used to constitute the staple of mountebank oratory'.

Menageries were travelling zoos. One of the better known was Wombwell's, which came to Herefordshire in May 1895 with its 500 birds and beasts, 'whose dens are entered and feats displayed by that most celebrated of all Animal Trainers (an Englishman of course), John Cooper'. Wombwell's went first to Leominster, then travelled via Pembridge and Weobley to Hereford, where it stopped in High Town; the Wombwell's animals' feeding times were advertised, just as in a zoo. The animals were best treated with care. The *Hereford Times* reported one cautionary tale in 1859: 'a few days ago one of the visitors at Wombwell's Menagerie in Halifax amused himself by insulting the elephant; when the animal, watching his opportunity, got the offender round the neck with his trunk, and held him up to the roof. An alarm was given to the keeper, who sternly asked the elephant "What's that about?" The animal then dropped his terrified guest as unceremoniously as if he had been a hot potato. The poor fellow alighted on his feet, but had to stagger back several paces before he could regain his perpendicular'.

As time went by circuses became larger and larger, and an odd kind of bidding war developed as to which circus was the biggest and best. One of the most gigantic of all was the Greatest Show on Earth, run by Barnum and Bailey Ltd, but the title was hotly disputed by Lord George Sanger, who announced in the *Hereford Journal* in 1894 that 'Barnum and Bailey, and the so-called Greatest Show on Earth is outdone and completely eclipsed by the newly organized invention of Lord George Sanger'. His own circus was 'the largest exhibition that ever moved upon the surface of the Earth', and 'any other exhibition in the world is as a mole hill to a mountain compared to this establishment'.

The Greatest Show on Earth came to Hereford in 1899. Held on a glorious mid-June Day, it was quite mind-boggling in its size and organisation. The villages for miles around emptied as people flocked to see it, and an astonishing 15,000 people bought tickets in the afternoon, with another 10,000 in the evening. On the morning of the show, the entire circus went on a grand procession through the streets of Hereford to the racecourse, taking half an hour to pass a given spot. The procession was led by 40 bay horses, controlled by one man, drawing a carriage containing a band. Then came the wild beasts in their special cages or carriages—tigers, lions, hyenas, bears, wolves, with keepers in each cage—followed by a caravan of camels with Arab and Sudanese riders, and behind them 20 performing elephants. The procession wound its way to the racecourse, where the marquees were set up, one for the menagerie,

THREE HORNED STEER

Exhibits from
'The Greatest Show on Earth'

and another for the 'prodigies' who included Hassan Ali, an Egyptian 7 feet 11 inches tall; a Hindu dwarf only 22 inches tall and weighing 24 pounds; a Lightning Calculator, who could solve almost any mathematical problem immediately; and Tomasso, the Human Pin-Cushion.

The prize for originality, however, must surely go to the Sanger Circus, whose elephants took part in a football match in Leominster in May 1900, with the centre forward elephant competing against the captain of the Leominster Football Club (see illustration opposite).

The market towns in the county all had their may fairs and mop, or hiring, fairs, with their accompanying penny gaffs or penny peep-shows, barrel organs, displays and merry-go-rounds. At least in earlier days odd bands of itinerant players might turn up at provincial fairs to perform some of the popular successes of the period, or older plays based on folk tales. The Hereford Theatre would now and again open for the May Fair.

They were always noisy. On 24 May 1824 the *Hereford Weekly Reporter* commented that it had been 'a busy week for Broad Street, the fine show of our county's cattle etc … was succeeded by a motley train of exhibitions who commenced their warfare on Wednesday with the deafening clangor of drums, trumpets, barrel organs, and vociferations broad and loud enough to stun the ear. Yet all the muted clamours and novelties surrounding our theatre did not in the least lessen its attraction'.

The gap left by the demolition of the theatre in 1857 was filled, at fair time, by itinerant players of variable talent. The *Hereford Times* ridiculed a troupe of actors at the 1858 May Fair, while the other attractions were little better:

GREAT BRITISH VICTORY !!

THE GREATEST SUCCESS ON EARTH.

WATERWORKS FIELD, LEOMINSTER,
WEDNESDAY, MAY 2nd, 1900.

LORD JOHN SANGER & SONS,

(Limited), Royal Circus, Hippodrome, Menagerie & Museum.

|| THE GREAT FOOTBALL MATCH—

ELEPHANT v. MAN

Wonderful piece of Animal Training. Great Football Match for a Massive Goblet, which will be on view at Mr. Bassett's, Tailor, South Street. Mr. Sid Phillips, Captain of the Leominster Football Club, has agreed to compete against Sanger's famed centre forward Elephant, as to which can kick the most goals out of five tries each. Mr. Phillips and the Elephant will keep goal in turn, and can only be seen at

LORD JOHN SANGER & SONS, Ltd., ROYAL CIRCUS.

NOVELTIES—Overflowing with Novelties.

The Great Military Drama, BOER OR BRITON? depicting in realistic accuracy incidents of the White Flag, revealing in Living Pictures the heroism of the British and Colonial Troops, and the dauntless courage of the Volunteers. Brave men do brave deeds. The leading papers of London and the Provinces say :—" A truly wonderful and realistic sight, and one we feel certain has never been equalled in this or any other country."

The whole of this vast addition will be exhibited daily : Afternoon at 2.30 ; Evening at 7.45.

Cheap Tickets will be issued by the Railway Co. from KINGTON, TITLEY, PEMBRIDGE, PRESTEIGN, BROMYARD, ROWDEN MILL, and FENCOTE Stations, returning after the performance. For Times and Fares see small Bills.

The pleasure fair was among the largest ever held in the city both in regard to the stock fair and the supply and demand of pleasure mongers and pleasure seekers.

The drama was represented by a dilapidated concern, with a 'company of artistes' who appeared as though they had suffered largely during the late monetary crisis and were not yet recovered from the effects. The talent displayed by these wandering Thespians was not of the most brilliant character. The 'dramas' were chiefly of the 'mysterious' school, with no particular plot but plenty of incident in the shape of terrific combats, ghostly visitations etc., the general effect being much aided by a profuse display of coloured fire, which is indispensable on such occasions, and never fails to excite great admiration among the spectators.

... The equestrian establishments on the ground were well patronised by a crowd of persons who had evidently made up their minds to be amused, although the class of entertainments presented was not such as would have satisfied an habitue of Astleys. The peep shows and galleries of art were well patronised by the juveniles, who were also extensive purchasers of those specimens of high art which are to be found in the possession of stall holders on such occasions.

As the 19th century wore on, fairs diminished in size and importance. In 1883 the *Leominster News* reported that the Wigmore fair was far smaller than in previous years; the attractions were 'of the most meagre description, comprising a penny show, a boxing booth, a few shooting galleries and stalls, and the inevitable revolving horses'. It was the same in Bromyard, where in 1898 the fair contained just a few penny booths and Punch and Judy shows; 15 or 20 years before stalls and merry-go-rounds had extended all the way down Church Street.

From the 1890s travelling showmen began to bring bioscope and electrograph shows to the fairs, both forms of early animated pictures. A few of the better known showmen—Messrs. Haggar, Crighton, and Strickland—used to come to Hereford for the May Fair.

CHAPTER XIII
Into the Cinema Age

The showmen who brought their bioscopes and animated pictures to the fairs soon began to give their shows in halls. In Ledbury, the Royal Hall, an annexe to the Royal Hotel, was used for very early cinematograph shows, and in 1900 was advertising its electrograph which was said to be 'absolutely the only projector of Edison's Famous Animated Photographs that gives a beautiful clear life-size picture without flickering'. A few years later, in 1910, it was showing a biodrama, *The Great Detective*. By this time, in most towns, halls were being adapted to show the new animated pictures. In December 1900 the Drill Hall in Hereford was used for an animated picture show featuring scenes from the Boer War. This was known as the Pooleograph—'the Finest Living Picture Machine ever invented', shown to the accompaniment of mandolin, orchestral and military bands.

The Drill Hall, however, was generally used for live entertainment. In October 1910 it was advertising *The Gay Gordons*, 'the greatest musical comedy ever seen in or out of London'. The advertisement below in the *Hereford Journal* announced that 'the Garrick Theatre will open as a High Class Picture Palace, with the latest singing and talking pictures'; the first night would consist of selections from the opera *Faust*, containing 'dramatic scenes faithfully portrayed by artists of the highest operatic skill, and synchronised with the finest reproductions of the human voice'.

Other performances at the Drill Hall in 1910 included, in January, Ian Robertson's London company in *The Passing of the Third Floor Back*. In this play, a mystical melodrama by Jerome K. Jerome, highly celebrated at the time, an enigmatic 'stranger' transforms a motley collection of louche characters, residents of a Bloomsbury lodging-house, by revealing to them their better selves. The 'stranger' had originally been played by Sir Johnston Forbes-Robertson, and in this Hereford

An advert for The Passing of the Third Floor Back, *with Ian Robertson, at the Drill Hall, printed for use as a postcard*

production was played by Ian Robertson (*see above*). A more familiar figure—to us—also appearing at the Drill Hall in 1910 was Ernest Shackleton, who came to give a lecture on his polar explorations. In October of the same year the Hereford Amateur Operatic Society used the hall to stage a performance of Grundy and Sullivan's *Haddon Hall.*

By 1911 the Garrick was advertised as 'the Home of Pictures', and soon it was used largely as a cinema, with live shows now and again. One of these was *Motoring*, 'the sketch that made Her Majesty cry – with laughter – at the Royal Command Performance at the Palace Theatre in London'. This was in 1914, by which time the theatre had changed its name to the New Garrick, 'the most up-to-date theatre in the city'.

The Hereford Corn Exchange had never made a very satisfactory theatre, and in 1910 the Corn Exchange Committee decided that the

The Corn Exchange and revamped Kemble: right, the façade (Derek Foxton Collection) and below the interior

building should be revamped to create a proper theatre, to be named the Kemble. Designs were drawn up by the architects Groom and Bettingham, and after much hard work the necessary sum of £5,000 was raised. The premises to the rear, consisting of livery stables facing onto Aubrey Street, were bought and the building extended by 18ft., giving a total length of 86ft. The hall was given raked seating, and a balcony built at the east end, with its own entrance; the proscenium arch was reconstructed,

shutters fitted to the glass roof lights, the stage extended—the new stage was 45ft. wide and 30ft. deep—dressing rooms built, and the entrance remodelled. It was an ambitious undertaking, and succeeded largely thanks to the persistence of one member of the Corn Exchange Committee, Mr. Jackson, who had devoted years of his life to the cause.

The new theatre was big enough to attract the major touring companies. It had seating for about 800 downstairs and another 200 or so in the balcony, the seats downstairs being removable so that the hall could still function as a Corn Exchange on Wednesdays. The plain walls of the old corn exchange were embellished with decorative plasterwork and painted rose pink, with a mahogany dado below; the proscenium arch was painted gold and given a red curtain. Below the theatre was a large basement available for use as a rifle range. It was an attractive theatre, but long and narrow, and its acoustics were more suited to music than to dialogue.

The Kemble Theatre opened in February 1911, just 125 years after the opening of its predecessor on the same site. The Kemble was longer than John Boles Watson's theatre, and wider because there was no pit passage and no carriageway to the side. But it was in the same spot that had seen John Philip Kemble's heroic nobility in *Hamlet*, and Sarah Siddons's passionate intensity in *Isabella*, as well as John Richer's tightrope walking, dragons breathing fire, and horses leaping around the stage in *Timour the Tartar*.

The opening play this time round was *The Pantomime Rehearsal*, performed in aid of the Hereford General Hospital. It starred Lady Evelyn Cotterell, who according to the *Hereford Times* possessed 'quite a strong penchant for theatricals', and her two sisters; the rest of the cast were equally prominent amateur actors and actresses. They were playing a group of incompetents

OPENING OF THE NEW

Kemble Theatre,

Broad Street Hereford.
—o—

IN AID OF THE HEREFORDSHIRE GENERAL HOSPITAL

LADY EVELYN COTTERELL

Will open the Kemble Theatre (under distinguished patronage) at the Corn Exchange, with

AMATEUR THEATRICALS
ON

THURSDAY & FRIDAY,
FEBRUARY 2nd & 3rd, 1911.
—o—

"The Pantomime Rehearsal."

The following Ladies and Gentlemen and others will take part:—

Lady Evelyn Cotterell	Mr. C. P. Little
Lady Helen Gordon Lennox	Colonel Ricardo
Lady Muriel Beckwith	Colonel Wood
Hon. Mrs. Francis Egerton	Captain C. Wood, D.S.O.
Hon. Mrs. C. Denison	Mr. G. A. Denny
Miss Evelyn Thornhill	

PRECEDED BY

"KITTY CLIVE."

By Lady Dorothy Lee Warner, Major Cox, and others.

MATINEE AT 2-30; EVENING PERFORMANCES AT 8.

ADMISSION :
EVENING PERFORMANCES, Thursday and Friday, Feb, 2nd and 3rd; at Popular Prices—Reserved Seats (numbered), 4s.; Second Seats, 3s.; Third Seats, 2s. and 1s. MATINEE, Thursday, February 2nd - Reserved Seats (numbered), 7s. 6d.; Balcony, 6s.; Second Seats, 5s.; Third Seats, 2s. 6d. and 2s.
Plan at Messrs. Heins & Co., Ltd., where seats can be booked. Tickets may be obtained of Messrs. Heins & Co., Ltd., Broad-street, and Messrs. Wilson & Phillips, Eign-street. 478

trying to rehearse for a pantomime, or as the *Hereford Times* put it, 'a band of really clever amateurs impersonating a set of comparative noodles with astonishing realism'.

Initially the Kemble was used for a mixture of plays and operas—including some by local amateur companies—and 'high class animated pictures'. The performers who had previously had to use the Drill Hall now came to the Kemble instead, and in its early years it saw the Carl Rosa Opera Company, numerous minstrel shows, and, in 1914, Sir Henry Irving.

On 7 April 1916 tragedy struck the Garrick Theatre when fire broke out during a charity concert for the troops, and eight young girls taking part in the show were burnt to death when the cotton wool dresses they were wearing caught fire. The curtain had just been lowered on a snow scene when the audience heard screams and a cry of 'fire'; they all started clambering over seats in their eagerness to reach the exit, the police appealed for calm, and the orchestra started playing. Two or three performers then jumped from the stage into the orchestra pit, and as they did so flames could be seen on stage. Mothers rushed round to the stage to find their children running about in flames. The fire spread quickly, despite all the precautions that had been taken when the theatre was built, and soon the building was entirely gutted. As a memorial to the

The Garrick after the fire (Helen Wallace and the Derek Foxton Collection)

119

eight girls who had lost their lives, the Mayor opened a memorial appeal in aid of the children's ward of the Herefordshire General Hospital. The memorial would 'commemorate a terrible event in our history, and be a permanent expression of sympathy with the parents of the immortal dead; and it will also confer a great service on our hospital, whose needs are always and ever urgent and pressing'.

After this tragedy, the theatre was reconstructed by its owner, Reginald Maddox, with improved facilities. The fare was still a mixture of films, plays and variety, but with an increasing proportion of films; by 1929 the Garrick was used almost entirely as a cinema. In November 1929 it showed the first talkie in Hereford, *Broadway Melody*. The Kemble provided a similar mixture of films and plays. In 1925 it was used for the Herefordshire Pageant (see illustration on p.122), an entertainment staged by local W.I.s, consisting of famous scenes from the county's history.

Gradually, though, live performances decreased as films became increasingly popular. In these early days of cinema, reels generally lasted for no more than 11 minutes or so, and cinemas would have two projectors, used alternately to provide a seamless film. Films, until the days of talkies, were generally shown with a musical accompaniment, consisting sometimes of a single instrumentalist, but usually a small orchestra of violin, trumpet, trombone, double bass, and percussion. In between films entertainment would be provided, in the form of clowns, jugglers or other performers.

Meanwhile, Hereford by now had another theatre, the Palladium, in Berrington Street. This building, now the Regal Bingo Hall, has had a long and chequered history. Originally built in 1787 as the Countess of Huntingdon's Chapel, in 1885 it was converted into the Beethoven Hall, a piano and parlour organ showroom for Messrs. Heins. When this moved to other premises in 1913, the building was converted into a cinema, and renamed the Picture House; in 1919 it was sold again, and this time renamed the Palladium Theatre. Seating 470, the Palladium had an unusual layout owing to the cramped locality of the building, and patrons unexpectedly entered the auditorium half way along its length.

In 1928 and 1929 the Palladium, under its manager Montague Franklin, underwent extensive alterations; the façade was redecorated and given a canopy, and the building extended by 18ft. in order to enlarge the stage to a width of 30ft. and a depth of 21ft., and enabling the building of five new dressing rooms at the back. The orchestra pit was sunk below floor level (the orchestra, incidentally, comprised a piano, a cornet, a violin, a cello, and a clarinet), and new seats were installed, with a raised balcony at the rear; the walls were given panels with floral

The Palladium in Berrington Street, showing its canopy erected in 1929, formerly the Countess of Huntingdon's Chapel and now the Regal Bingo Hall

designs. The lighting was greatly improved; and, as a final touch, a room was provided for the accommodation of perambulators. The renovated theatre now seated about 600. It was still to be used mainly as a cinema, but with live performances every two or three weeks. The first performance in the revamped theatre, in March 1930, was the eighth annual Community Theatre Festival, in which 26 one-act plays were presented, 13 given by teams of Women's Institutes, and 13 by amateur dramatic societies.

In the early 1930s both the Kemble and the Garrick were bought by Union Cinemas. The Kemble was to focus on live entertainment and was extensively remodelled; the ceiling was replaced and the interior decorated in Art Deco style. The *Hereford Times* reported that 'the seating arrangements will generally be on a par with, if not better than, those of the best West End theatres of London, and the keynote of the decorative scheme generally will be a new marvellous coloured lighting system, in which it will be found that Hereford is leading the way in this country'. The proscenium arch was altered, the stage rebuilt, and the entrance altered to include a canopy with neon sign. The changes were

HEREFORDSHIRE FEDERATION of WOMENS' INSTITUTES

HEREFORDSHIRE PAGEANT

GIVEN BY THE MEMBERS OF THE HEREFORDSHIRE
FEDERATION OF WOMEN'S INSTITUTES IN THE

Kemble Theatre, Oct. 22, 23 & 24, 1925

. . . .

Episodes from County History

Produced by Lt.-Col. J. L. SLEEMAN, C.M.G., C.B.E., M.V.O., M.A.

PROLOGUE : Verses written by The
Rev. Canon Arthur T. Bannister, M.A.

MUSIC suitable to the date of each
Episode under the direction of Miss Hovil.

The Chronicle———Miss Drusilla Foster.

not universally popular, one critic complaining that the traditional lines
of the proscenium arch were 'replaced by a form more suited to a pagan
temple'; and the canopy undoubtedly did little to enhance the fine
façade of the old Corn Exchange.

Looking back, an aged theatregoer remembered some of the more
unusual shows between the wars: 'Two variety shows remain in my
memory; one, a one-armed motorcyclist, clad in a white boiler suit,

A MASQUE

OF

HEREFORDSHIRE

MYTHS AND LEGENDS

Presented by the
Herefordshire Federation of Women's Institutes

In

The CATHEDRAL CLOISTERS

(by kind permission of the Custos and Vicars Choral)

Devised, Collected and Written by
THE HON. MRS. DUNNE.

Master of the Masque
COLONEL J. L. SLEEMAN, C.B., C.M.G., C.B.E., M.V.O.

coaxing his machine (a velocette, I fancy) in and around a series of obstacles; no mean feat in that less than spacious stage. The other recollection is of a gent in evening dress persuading a flight of reluctant cockatoos into firing miniature cannon'.

In 1935 ambitious celebrations were organised in Hereford to mark the centenary of Sarah Siddons's death. In a 20th-century counterpart to John Crisp's 1816 Garrick centenary celebrations, a luncheon was given at the Town Hall by the mayor, F. Lewis Smith, and the chief steward, T.S. Arkwright, with descendants of the Siddons and Kemble families as guests of honour. After the luncheon, a tablet was unveiled in Church Street by a descendant, Mrs. Siddons-Budgen, and a chronicle play was

The Garrick in use as the County A.R.P. Headquarters
during the Second World War (Philip Cowal and the Derek Foxton Collection)

performed at the Kemble Theatre, written by a local writer, R.E. Abbott, and including a number of Siddons descendants among the amateur cast.

In the following year, 1936, Union Cinemas was bought by Associated British Cinemas, owners of the Garrick. In 1938, A.B.C. Cinemas built the Ritz Cinema in Commercial Road, closing the Garrick at the same time. (During the war the building was used as the A.R.P. headquarters and as a training film establishment; it also housed the county library). The Ritz now showed all the best films, and the Kemble showed those which would formerly have appeared at the Garrick, with the films still alternating with plays and other live performances.

In 1939 Derek Salberg, manager of the Alexandra Theatre in Birmingham, came to an agreement with Montague Franklin, now the owner of the Palladium, and set up a repertory company at the theatre. Salberg came from a theatrical family; his brother Reggie was manager of the Wolverhampton Theatre, and a cousin managed another theatre in the Midlands. Salberg was a generous and popular man; a member of one of his repertory companies recalled a time when 'the wife of a company member was in dire need of an operation, the cost of which was estimated at £100. In trepidation the actor approached Derek Salberg and asked if he would consider lending him the money. When Salberg enquired how his employee would repay him the actor suggested that an amount might be deducted from his wages on a weekly basis, a proposal that Salberg agreed to. Imagine the actor's surprise upon opening his pay packet to find that his salary was exactly the same as it had always been, and that the expected deficit had been swallowed up in a pay rise'.

Salberg's producer at the Palladium was Donald Finley, who was to return to the repertory company at a later date. It was a difficult time to start such a venture, and by 1942, because of wartime difficulties, the theatre had reverted to showing films. After the war, in 1946, Salberg bought the Palladium outright, renaming it the County Theatre, and reformed his repertory company. The County Theatre Players, as they were called, numbered 15, the best known among them being Arthur Lowe. Other members in 1946 included Nancy Roberts, who had been instrumental in reviving the repertory movement after the war. 'No more popular actress has ever strode the stage of the theatre', wrote the *Hereford Times* in 1950, 'and her cheery personality, as well as her great acting ability, should contribute largely to placing the cast in high favour' (she was later to become well known on television as Granny Fagg in the *Grove Family*, a BBC serial of the sixties). The opening play at the County, on 6 January 1947, was *How Are They at Home?* by J.B. Priestley.

Newcomers for the 1950 season included Colin Laurence, one of Salberg's stalwarts from Wolverhampton and Birmingham; Paul Morgan; and John Melvin, 'a highly promising juvenile whose brilliant acting in the production of *Peace Comes to Peckham* in 1948 at the County Theatre is still remembered'. The 1950 season was made up mostly of recent West End productions: *The Happiest Days of your Life*, by John Dighton, Daphne Du Maurier's *September Tide*, Eric Lintlaker's farcical *Love in Albania*, and a well-known melodrama, *Maria Marten*.

In its short life as a repertory theatre, the County attracted quite a number of well-known actors; as well as Arthur Lowe and

Donald Finlay, it saw Beryl Johnstone, Christopher Bond and Richard Leach. 'Hereford is particularly fortunate', wrote the *Hereford Times* in 1950, 'to have what has come to be regarded as one of the best provincial repertory theatres in the whole of England, as well as, of course, another live theatre [the Kemble] which is also doing excellent work in the variety world. Very few places of a similar size can have two such theatres and this tremendous asset, not only from the point of view of the citizens, but of the visitors, is one which should be retained at all costs'.

Nationally, however, repertory theatre was struggling. The 1950 season attracted small audiences, and at the end of the year the County

126

Theatre, under Miles Byrne, its recently appointed managing director, reverted to productions by touring companies, among them the Young Vic Company's production of *The Merchant of Venice*, operas performed by the Roy Taylor Opera Company; and a production of *The Beggar's Opera*. After a few years of small, if loyal, audiences, in 1953 Salberg sold the County Theatre to Miles Byrne, who had by now also leased the Kemble. Byrne decided to use the County largely as a cinema, and installed a succession of new cinema technologies—wide-screen, 3-D and Cinemascope. The films were interspersed with live shows, and Byrne managed to run several repertory seasons there. In June 1957, however, with audiences disappointingly thin, Byrne finally decided to close the County Theatre, which was to reopen in November as the County Ballroom. In this new incarnation as a ballroom, roller-skating rink, and later a restaurant-cabaret, it lasted until July 1962, when it reverted to its former use as a theatre and cinema, under yet another name, the Regal. This in turn lasted for about three years, until in June 1965 the building was turned into the Regal Bingo Hall; it has remained as such for an unprecedented 35 years.

Myles Byrne was hoping to use the Kemble for live theatre, and in 1953 arranged for Derek Salberg to bring another repertory company to play there for a four-week season. Salberg's company was composed of

KEMBLE THEATRE

HEREFORD.

Thursday, Friday & Saturday, March 18th, 19th & 20th, at 7-45. MATINEE SATURDAY, at 2-15

THE INEZ HOWARD COMPANY

Under the direction of

HENRY CHATTELL,

By arrangement with

IDA MOLESWORTH AND TEMPLER POWELL,

PRESENT

WHITE CARGO

By LEON GORDON.

Based on the Novel " Hell's Playground," by Ida Vera Simonton.

The Sensational Success from the Playhouse and Princes Theatres, London.

Characters in the Play :

The Doctor	...	GUS WHEATMAN
Jim Fish	...	... S. ROSSITER
Weston (the Man who stays)...	...	HENRY CHATTELL
Ashley (the Man who goes home)	...	SHAUN LANGFORD
The Missionary	...	HUGH MONTGOMERY
The Skipper	...	JACK DENTON
The Engineer	...	DENNIS AYMOND
Langford	...	BALLARD BERKELEY
Tondeleyo	...	RANI WALLER
Worthing	...	WILSON RAYNE

The action of the Play takes place in a Bungalow on the West Coast of Africa.

ACT I—SCENE I. ...	...	AN AFTERNOON IN DECEMBER
„ II. ...	...	... THAT NIGHT
ACT II—SCENE I. ...	...	EIGHT MONTHS LATER
„ II. ...	...	THREE MONTHS LATER
ACT III—SCENE I. ...	...	ONE YEAR LATER
„ II. ...	...	A FEW MONTHS LATER

During each Act the Curtain will be lowered momentarily to denote the passing of time.

Manager		CLAUD AYMOND
Stage Director		JACK DENTON
Carpenter		J. B. HUMPHRYS

Cast of a play on the stage at the Kemble, with a backdrop of High Town with the old Market Hall (Derek Foxton Collection)

successful members of his other repertory companies, including Ian Cunningham, who had been at the County, and Gerald Cuff, who Salberg considered 'one of the most promising young actors in the country today'. The Kemble was now showing films for three nights a week, with a play on one night a week. Keen to save money, Byrne employed one manager—Reg Greenway—to run both the Kemble and the County, and on film nights Greenway's job involved switching projectors and changing the reels in both cinemas—in those days reels only lasted for 11 minutes, and cinemas would have two projectors to enable films to be screened continuously. This meant that Greenway had to change the reel in one cinema, then hop onto his bicycle and pedal as fast as he could to the other in time to change the reel there; and so on until the films were finished. At least it must have kept him fit.

The Kemble was still used for a variety of other shows, such as wrestling, Savoy operas, and an annual pantomime. It still attracted, sometimes, big names—Gracie Fields, for example. On occasion a small ice rink was also installed on the stage, and in 1955 the basement was converted into a roller-skating rink. Times were difficult, though, for both theatres and cinemas. Audiences were declining, and the Kemble by this time was increasingly shabby and in a state of decay. It staggered on for a few more years until, after a final production of *Brigadoon* in the spring of 1962 by the Hereford Gilbert and Sullivan Society, the building was finally and tragically demolished in 1963.

After the demolition of the Kemble, and the closure of the Regal (formerly the Palladium) in 1965, Herefordshire was without a theatre. There were other venues, none of them totally satisfactory: in Hereford, the small Greenland's Hall, or YMCA Hall, in St. Owen Street; the Art and Blind Colleges; the hall of Belmont Abbey School; and the Garrison Theatre at Bradbury Lines (from 1948 until 1972, when security restrictions prevented further use); in Bromyard the former British Legion Hall, and in Ross the Roxy Cinema.

The Herefordshire Arts Association, formed soon after the demolition of the Kemble, floated the idea of another, smaller, theatre for Hereford. Finally, in 1970 plans were drawn up for an arts centre, including a 250-seat theatre, to be built at 25 and 27 St. Owen Street, but costs soared and in 1974 the project was abandoned. When the county library, based in the old Garrick Theatre, closed in the same year, there was long debate over whether to convert the building, which still retained all its seats and other fittings, back into a theatre and arts centre, but finally, in 1978, it was demolished.

Another possible site presented itself with the closure in the late 1970s of the municipal swimming baths in Edgar Street. A small but determined group of four local societies—the Hereford Amateur Operatic Society, the Hereford Gilbert and Sullivan Society, the Hereford Players and the Wye Players—embarked on a scheme to convert the former baths into a theatre. An independent charitable trust was set up, an appeal launched to raise £100,000, a club established for supporters of the proposed theatre, and the conversion work went ahead, carried out in large part by hard-working volunteers, with many of the materials donated by local firms. The pool was filled in, a sloping floor created for the raked seating, and a proscenium arch and stage, 30ft. wide and 24ft. deep, constructed. Dressing rooms and rehearsal rooms were built, and a bar and restaurant created at the front of the building. The amateur operatic societies wanted a large theatre, and the amateur dramatic societies a small theatre; the result was a compromise, with the new theatre containing 350 seats. The seats themselves had been saved from the former Garrick Theatre before its demolition, together with plaster mouldings from the Garrick's proscenium arch which were also installed in the new theatre. In 1979 the former baths reopened as the Nell Gwynne Theatre and Arts Centre.

The Nell Gwynne was used by a mixture of touring professional companies and local amateur societies, and in 1982, after some modifi-

The NELL GWYNNE Theatre

cations to the interior, it started to show films as well, at a time when the future of Hereford's cinemas was in doubt. The theatre was dependent on a large team of dedicated volunteers who manned the box office, staffed the bar, and did other vital jobs. However, with audience numbers often disappointing, the theatre's financial position became increasingly difficult; finally in 1984 it became insolvent and was forced to close. The city council instead leased the theatre to Stan Stennett, entertainer and star of *Crossroads*. Stennett, who lived in Cardiff, already ran The Roses Theatre in Tewkesbury with the help of his two sons. With extra funding from Hereford City Council, the Nell Gwynne reopened, on 1 April 1985, as the New Hereford Theatre, and Stennett appointed Mike Tomkins, chairman of the Hereford Amateur Operatic Society, as manager.

Under this new regime the theatre continued for a few years. In 1989, now with another manager, a studio theatre was added for the use of youth groups, smaller productions and workshops. But although the council's grant increased inexorably year after year, the New Hereford Theatre faced the same problems of sparse audiences and lack of funds which had led to the demise of the Nell Gwynne. When Stennett's lease ran out in June 1994 the city council decided to take over the running of the theatre itself. A newly appointed artistic director, Jonathan Stone, was put in charge, and the building renamed the Hereford Theatre and Arts Centre. Meanwhile, it became increasingly clear that the fabric of the building was in poor condition, and that extensive refurbishment would be needed in order to bring it up to public entertainment licence standards; a better alternative would be to replace the existing theatre with a purpose-built arts centre. The city council gave a grant of £200,000 towards this new project, and an application was made to the National Lottery, one of the first such applications in the region. The application was successful, and the lottery commission awarded a grant of £3.75 million towards the new venue, and this was supplemented by private fundraising. The next stage was to design a suitable building, for which a competition was held, administered by the RIBA; the winner was a Birmingham architect, Glenn Howells.

The Hereford Theatre and Arts Centre closed its doors at the end of March 1996, and demolition began in April 1997. In its place rose a sleek modern building, The Courtyard Centre for the Arts, which officially opened in September 1998 with performances of *Cabaret*, *Bugsy Malone* and *Shading The Crime*, performed by The Courtyard Community Company, The Courtyard Youth Theatre and New Theatre Works respectively. Among the cast in *Cabaret* was Geoff Alcock, who had the unusual distinction of having appeared in the last performance at the Kemble before its demolition in 1963, as well as in the first show in the newly converted Nell Gwynne Theatre in 1979.

Classed as a mid-scale venue, The Courtyard contains a theatre, seating 434, and a smaller studio theatre, seating 126, a rehearsal room (the Garrick Room), meeting rooms and exhibition spaces, as well as a spacious foyer, with bar and restaurant areas. The Main House has removable seating in the stalls, enabling the space to be used for craft shows and other events; the studio theatre is used for experimental work, new writing, and generally for smaller shows. Both theatres also have projection equipment. In its early years The Courtyard had to contend with not just a certain amount of criticism of its design but also problems caused by water, which as well as leaking through the flat roof also began to well up from underground because of a higher than expected water table; one early performance had to be delayed when water started to seep into the orchestra pit as the show was about to begin. Despite these early teething troubles, The Courtyard has quickly become a lively focal point for artistic activity in Herefordshire.

CHAPTER XIV
Theatres, Companies and
Amateur Dramatic Societies

This last chapter describes the various theatres, theatre companies and performers, professional and amateur, based in Herefordshire today. For reasons of space it confines itself to the larger and more established groups, though there are many other smaller village-based societies which cannot really be encompassed, sadly, in a book of this length.

The Conquest Theatre in Bromyard, built in 1991, was the brainchild of the Bromyard and District Amateur Drama Group. Founded before the war, the group's performances originally took place in the Public Hall in New Road, and then from 1978 in the former British Legion Hall, a corrugated iron building in Old Road converted into a theatre using items cleverly scavenged from various sources: a maple floor from an old gymnasium, seats from the Regal Cinema in Tenbury, and the curtain from the Gaumont Cinema in Worcester. The hall was far from ideal, though; it was too hot to use in the summer, and the leaks in the roof became ever worse. Rather than attempting to repair the hall, ambitious plans were drawn up for a new purpose-built theatre, and after generous donations from the council and from private sources, a site was bought and an impressive new 150-seat theatre built.

The Conquest Theatre is used by professional touring companies, as well as by other amateur societies. Its own drama group currently produces four plays a year, and apart from these the theatre has been used for an enormous range of shows from jazz and folk bands, through opera, tap dancers, Japanese drummers, clairvoyants and faith healers to falconry displays.

The Courtyard Centre for the Arts, in Hereford, has become a lively arts centre, its programme catering for all tastes with a mixture of theatre, films, music, opera, dance, exhibitions and other activities. As well as attracting a wide variety of professional actors and other performers—including Susannah York, the Reduced Shakespeare Company, the Edinburgh Puppet Company, Bob Geldof, taiko drummers, Lindisfarne and the English String Orchestra, to name a few—The Courtyard provides a suitable venue for local amateur societies. It has spawned a number of its own theatre companies, such as **The Courtyard Community Company**, made up of professional and amateur performers which stages regular performances directed by the Courtyard's Artistic Director, Jonathan Stone; as well as **New Theatre Works**, a professional company formed in 1999 to perform new texts in the theatre and to devise works using less conventional venues such as buses, rivers and family centres); **The Courtyard Youth Theatre**, and **The Courtyard Senior Youth Theatre**, not to mention their in-house contemporary dance outfit, **2FaCeD DaNcE Company**. Every March The Courtyard also hosts the Herefordshire County Drama Festival, now in its 65th year. The first stage of the All-England Theatre Festival, this provides an opportunity for local societies to compete in staging one-act plays.

The **Eardisley Little Theatre Company** has an enviable record of awards at the All-England Theatre Festival; it has won the regional competition every year for the last five years—most recently for an adaption of *The Caucasian Chalk Circle*—and in 2000 reached the national finals with a performance of *Blue Remembered Hills.* These recent successes are in large part attributable to an enthusiastic director, and as well as winning competitions the performances have engendered a great community spirit.

Founded 27 years ago, the Eardisley Little Theatre Company has around 45 active members, and a youth group whose masked performance of *Hansel and Gretel* also won an award at the 2002 festival. Every summer the company performs an extended version of its festival entry in the open air in Eardisley, and in the winter stages a pantomime in Eardisley village hall. Other recent performances have included *The Canterbury Tales* and *The Withered Arm*, an adaption of a story by Thomas Hardy, as well as various Ayckbourn plays such as *Gosforth's Fete* and *Third Person Singular.*

The **Hereford Amateur Operatic Society** (HAOS), founded in 1898, is the third oldest surviving amateur dramatic society in the country. The impetus for its formation came from a group of Savoy Opera enthusiasts

Front cover of Hereford Amateur Operatic Society's programme for
La Cage Aux Folles, *November 2000*

Front cover of Hereford Amateur Operatic Society's programme for
My Fair Lady, *November 2001*

who staged a performance of *The Sorcerer* in the Drill Hall, in Friar Street, in 1898. From 1904 the society put on annual performances, still mainly of Savoy Operas, at the Drill Hall and then, from 1911, in the newly built Kemble Theatre. Productions went into abeyance during the Second World War, but restarted in 1947 with a production of *The Belle of New York* at the County Theatre (as the Palladium was now called). Most performances were still of musical plays and operettas, though not now limited to the Savoy Operas. In 1960 the American musical arrived in the form of *Oklahoma* by Rodgers and Hammerstein, performed by the society in that year. Until the 1970s directors were generally brought in from outside the society, but from then on most of its productions were directed in-house, but with a professional orchestra. After the demolition of the Kemble the society faced the common problem of where to perform. In the late 1970s HAOS acquired its own premises in the shape of the former Holy Trinity Church Hall in Whitecross Road; renamed the Operatic Hall, it provided a suitable venue for rehearsals, youth theatre and smaller productions.

Recent productions, now of course at The Courtyard, and always well supported, have included *The Wizard of Oz*, *South Pacific*, *My Fair Lady*, and *Carousel*.

The **Hereford Amateur Pantomime Society** originated in 1963 as the Wiggins Pantomime. Early in the 1960s Wiggins, newly moved down from Scotland, used to send all its employees' children to the annual pantomime at the Kemble Theatre. When the Kemble was demolished in 1963, the Wiggins staff were faced with the sad prospect of hundreds of disappointed children. The Wiggins Recreation Club, which already had a flourishing drama group, decided instead to try staging its own pantomimes in the canteen. The first of the Wiggins Pantomimes was *Ali Baba*, staged on two Saturdays in February 1964; it was a great success, and the pantomimes became an annual event, the number of performances increasing steadily year by year until they were running for a fortnight in January and February. To begin with the canteen could seat as many as 700, but when staging was put in the number of seats was reduced to 579. Every year the performances were sold out, even though for the first few years they were only open to Wiggins staff and their children.

In 1981 the Wiggins canteen was sold, and if the pantomimes were to continue they would have to find a new venue. The group decided to reconstitute itself as the Hereford Amateur Pantomime Society, and since the link with Wiggins had gone the new society was open to everyone. The 1983 pantomime, *Mother Goose*, was performed in the

Royal National College for the Blind, but since 1998 the pantomimes have been at The Courtyard.

Today the society has around 120 members, mostly families, and including many grandchildren of the original founders. Recent pantomimes have included *Dick Whittington, Sinbad the Sailor,* and *Goldilocks and The Three Bears.* Each year the profits from the show have been donated to a local charity.

The **Hereford Gilbert and Sullivan Operatic Society** was founded in 1948 by former members of the Hereford Amateur Operatic Society who preferred to stick to the Savoy Operas when the Amateur Operatic Society began to widen its repertoire. The G & S Society does sometimes, however, perform other operas as well. Its performances used to take place at the Kemble Theatre, including *Brigadoon,* the last performance before the theatre's demolition in 1963. Recent performances have included *The Mikado, Merrie England,* and *The Gondoliers.* The G & S Society has also performed in Hereford's German twin, Dillenberg, and is planning a visit to Vierzon, the city's French twin.

The **Hereford Players** were founded in 1945. Until recently they used to put on three performances a year, usually at the Greenland's Hall, as well as entering the Herefordshire County Drama Festival, going through a few times to the third round. In 2001 they performed one play at The Courtyard, and entered two plays in the festival, one of which went through to the second round. The Hereford Players also have a youth group. Recent productions have included *Dark of the Moon* and *Cider with Rosie.*

The **Kingsland Amateur Theatrical Society** (KATS) is not, sadly, the same as the Kingsland Amateur Dramatic Society which flourished over a century ago. KATS was founded as the result of enthusiasm engendered by a WI competition, and the society's first production was *The Walrus and the Carpenter.* Every year a pantomime is staged in the village hall, and sometimes a spring show as well; there are also occasional performances by the society's youth group. Recent productions have included the pantomime *Snow White,* and a one-act comedy, *Last Tango in Little Grimley.*

The **Kington and District Operatic Society** was founded in about 1969 to perform Gilbert and Sullivan operas, one of which is staged every year in the autumn. By popular demand an annual pantomime has been added to the repertoire. The society is in a thriving state, with around 50 members. Since Kington now has no theatre, the Savoy Operas are performed at the Pavilion Theatre in Llandrindod Wells, but the annual pantomimes take place in the Kington Leisure Centre. Recent Savoy operas have included *The Mikado* and *HMS Pinafore*, and recent pantomimes *Jack and the Beanstalk* and *Dick Whittington.*

The **Ledbury Amateur Dramatic Society** (LADS) was founded in 1935 as the Ledbury Cine Society. Because many of its members enjoyed amateur dramatics as well as film-making, the society changed its name in 1938 to the Ledbury Amateur Dramatic and Cine Society, and in the same year its first play, *Tilly of Bloomsbury*, was produced in the Drill Hall. After the war the society moved temporarily to a makeshift theatre left by prisoners of war and then, when this was no longer available, to the Church Room. With a good deal of sweat the Church Room was converted into the Market Theatre, and at the same time the society was rechristened a second time as the Ledbury Amateur Dramatic Society. In the following years they regularly performed plays by Bernard Shaw, Noel Coward and Somerset Maugham. In 1986 disaster struck when the **Market Theatre** was gutted by fire, but was quickly rebuilt and reopened in 1987.

In the late 1990s plans where made to build a new theatre, and after lengthy fundraising efforts the 128-seat Market Theatre was opened in 2000. LADS performs three or so plays (sometimes staged in association with Pentabus) plus a pantomime each year, and the theatre is also used for professional productions—recent visitors include Hi Jinks and Taiko drummers from Japan—and films.

The **Leominster Theatre Company** was founded about 25 years ago as the Leominster Drama Group. In past years it has staged plays, such as *Hamlet* and *Rosencranz and Guildenstern are Dead*, at the Minster School and the Community Centre, as well as giving performances at the Leominster Festival, and occasionally staging Christmas entertainments at the Forbury Chapel, thereby reviving the old theatrical tradition of that building. More recently the Leominster Theatre Company has limited itself to monthly playreadings, but has plans to stage a production in the near future.

Mad Dogs Theatre Company was founded in about 1990, and puts on sometimes unusual productions in varied locations, often in schools, churches and village halls. Past productions have included *A Midsummer Night's Dream* in the garden of Treago, a mystery play at Dore Abbey (done as promenade theatre), *The Tempest*, also at Dore Abbey, *Monty*

Python's Quest for the Holy Grail, and *Talking Heads,* a touring production performed in villages throughout the county, and subsequently at The Courtyard.

Magna is based in Credenhill, near Hereford. The youngest of the Hereford societies, it was founded in 1980 and has about 40 members, including a youth group. It has always had a link with the Royal National College for the Blind in Hereford, where some Magna performances are held; most though now take place at The Courtyard. Magna usually stages two plays a year, as well as a pantomime and a performance given by the youth group. Recent productions have included *The Wind of Heaven, Pack of Lies, Bazaar and Rummage, A Midsummer Night's Dream* and *Cinderella.*

Pentabus, a professional theatre company, was founded in 1974 by West Midlands Arts with the aim of taking drama into rural communities by staging productions in schools and village halls. It is now one of the West Midlands' leading touring theatre companies. Pentabus concentrates particularly on performing work by new writers, by appointing writers-in-residence, running writing courses, collaborating with playwrights and also working with film and video makers. The company usually performs two or three plays each year, and recent productions have included *Peppering Over, Silent Engine,* and *Smashed Eggs,* a play for 8 to 11-year-olds which arose out of workshops with local children.

The **Ross Operatic and Amateur Dramatic Society** (ROADS) was founded in 1921, and to begin with its productions—mainly Savoy Operas in its early years—were staged in the New Theatre (formerly the Corn Exchange) in the High Street. One major drawback here was the cramped stage, with no means of getting from one side to the other behind the scenes. After exiting on one side, actors had to rush down the fire escape, then sprint along the road into the King's Head, up the stairs and through a door leading to the other side of the stage.

The Corn Exchange was destroyed in a fire in 1939. After a long period with no theatre—the Roxy Cinema, built in 1941, provided a venue of sorts—in 1971 the society bought the former fire station behind the Royal Hotel, and after a long drawn-out fundraising campaign converted it into the **Phoenix Theatre**, a small but attractive theatre with 65 seats, opened in 1983. With the help of a generous lottery grant the building has now been extended to provide extra space for a bar and new changing rooms; the auditorium, however, remains unchanged. ROADS generally puts on five plays a year, and recent productions have included *A Chorus of Disapproval, A Day in the Life of Joe Egg, Nude with Violin, Teechers, Percival the Performing Pig* and, to christen the newly enlarged theatre, a musical, *The Little Shop of Horrors.*

The Wye Theatre Company, based in Hereford, began life in the 1930s as the YMCA Players, so called because performances took place in the YMCA hall, or Greenland's Hall as it was also known, in St. Owen Street. A small hall, seating 250 or so, with a tiny stage, the Greenland's Hall saw productions by the YMCA Players of plays by Checkov, Ibsen, Tennesee Williams and Arthur Miller, alongside popular farces and comedies. When the hall was demolished in the 1970s and the connection with the YMCA severed, the society's name was conveniently shortened to the Wye Players. Now renamed the Wye Theatre Company, they have been performing one or two plays a year at The Courtyard. Recent productions have included *Under Milk Wood* and *Blythe Spirit.*

Bibliography

Brown, John Russell ed., *Oxford Illustrated History of the Theatre*, OUP, 1995

Denning, Anthony, ed. Ranger, Paul, *Theatre in the Cotswolds: The Boles Watson Family and the Cirencester Theatre*, London, 1993

Dallow, Margaret, compiler, *The Life and Times of the Conquest Theatre (so far)*, 2000

Dyer, Robert, *Nine Years of an Actor's Life*, London, 1833

George, David in *Records of Early English Drama newsletter*, vol 10 no 1, Toronto, 1985

Girouard, Mark, *Life in the English Country House*, Yale, 1978

Hannam-Clark, Theodore, *Drama in Gloucestershire*, London, 1928

Highfill, Philip H. jnr. *et al.*, *A Biographical Dictionary of Actors, Actresses, Musicians, Dancers, Managers and Other Stage Personnel in London 1660-1800*, Illinois, 1973

Holcroft, Thomas, *Memoirs of the late Thomas Holcroft, written by himself and continued to the time of his death, from his diary, notes and other papers*, ed. W. Hazlitt, London, 1816

Hornsey, Brian, *Ninety Years of Cinema in Hereford*, 1991

Hornsey, Brian, *Cinemas in North Herefordshire*

Howe, Miss, 'Address spoken by Miss Howe at her Benefit', *Hereford Tracts, no. 8*, 1818

Klausner, David, 'Research in Progress' in *Records of Early English Drama newsletter*, University of Toronto Press, 1979

Klausner, David, ed., *Records of Early English Drama—Herefordshire and Worcestershire*, Toronto, 1990

Leather, Ella Mary, *Folklore of Herefordshire*, London, 1973

McGregor-Hastie, Roger, *Nell Gwyn*, London, 1987

Manvill, Roger, *Sarah Siddons, Portrait of an Actress*, London, 1970

Marshall, Herbert and Stock, Mildred, *Ira Aldridge, the Negro Tragedian*, London, 1958

Mathews, Anne, *Memoirs of Charles Mathews, Comedian*, London, 1838-9

Mathews, Charles, *Mr. Mathews at Home*, London, 1830

Oman, Carola, *David Garrick*, London, 1994

Parry, Richard, *The History of Kington*, Kington, 1845

Price, Cecil, 'John Ward, Stroller' in *Theatre Notebook*, vol. 1 no. 1, 1941

Price, Cecil, 'Some Movements of the Bath Company 1729-1734', in *Theatre Notebook*, Oct. 1946

Price, Cecil, *The English Theatre in Wales*, Cardiff, 1948

Rees, W.J., *Hereford Guide*, Hereford, 1827

Reeve, N.C., *Town in the Marches*, Leominster, 1972

Ridley, Jasper, *The Freemasons*, London, 1999

Rowse, A.L., *Shakespeare the Man*, London, 1973

Skarratt, Thomas Carleton, *Diaries 1818-1909*, Kington, 1987

Sinclair, J.B., and Fenn, R.W.D., *The Border Janus. A New Kington History*, Kington, 1995

Strong, Roy, *The Spirit of Britain*, London, 1999

Trussler, Simon, *Cambridge Illustrated History of the British Theatre*, Cambridge, 1994

Tucker-Murray, John, *English Dramatic Companies 1558-1642*, London, 1910

Wilmott, Carl, 'The Theatre in Kington, Herefordshire', *Theatre Notebook*, vol. 5 no. 2, 1951

Winspear, Suz, *Worcester's Lost Theatre; the Story of the Worcester Theatre Royal*, Worcester, 1996

Newspapers & Magazines

Gloucester Journal
Hereford Journal
Hereford Times
Hereford Weekly Reporter, or Theatrical Looker-on, 1824
Notes & Queries, 1 (1868), 141-2, 206, CLX (1931), 301
Ross Gazette

Other records

Herefordshire playbills, 1791-1830, Herefordshire County Record Office

Ruth Bourne Diaries, Herefordshire County Record Office

Story of Nell Gwyn, Herefordshire County Record Office

Scrapbooks of amateur dramatic entertainments in Kington and Kingsland in the 1880s and 1890s, Hereford City Library

Various deeds relating to Hereford Corn Exchange, Derek Foxton

Index

In our Dreaming & Singing
The Story of the Three Choirs Festival Chorus
compiled by Barbara Young   £6.95

'Without Handel, England's opera houses and choral societies, organists and orchestras, even royal patronage and inclusion in the European musical scene, would have lacked a particular impetus. Also many a choir would have missed the annual musical treat and uplifting experience of singing one of the greatest pieces of music ever written—Messiah. Maybe choral societies would have evolved anyway, for the British do like to get together for a good sing. Those of us who feel self-conscious and pretend to have no voice when asked to sing solo, find we can unleash vocal chords for the Hallelujah Chorus. Indeed Handel did more for the singers of this country than can ever be measured.'

'The three organists at the time, Robinson, Lloyd and Sanders were very patient and persevering, but the work was a shock to the Three Choirs system. Spoken whisperings rising to hysterical crescendos, cocktail party conversations and a simulated Trafalgar Square demonstration against war were not regular Festival fare and we found it embarrassing to have to shout in the cathedral.'

Barbara Young, for several years a member of the Three Choirs Festival Chorus, explores the origins of that chorus and how it changed to meet the demands of musical taste through three centuries.

This is not a 'dry' book, but a very personal account which will appeal to listeners and singers alike. The story is told from the inside by one who has enjoyed the challenge of learning the greatest works of the choral repertoire, has known the problems posed by new pieces, rehearsed under difficult conditions and felt the excitement and exhilaration of taking part in some memorable performances. To help tell the tale, the author uses letters and anecdotes from chorus members past and present, and has included many engravings, drawings and photographs.